# HIGH ACRES
# MAPLE SYRUP
# COOK BOOK

By Susan Chapman Melanson

High Acres Maple Syrup
Oak Hill Farm
South Hiram, Maine

FIRST EDITION (PERFECT BOUND)

Copies just like this one, and also a spiral-bound edition, are available
through
www.lulu.com

COVER ARTWORK:
"Maple Huskies", an acrylic on canvas by Sue Melanson.

ISBN 978-0-6151-4506-8

# TABLE OF CONTENTS

3

Frozen Desserts (Including Ice Cream)
Pies and Crisps
Puddings and Mousses
Miscellaneous Desserts

# CHAPTER 1
## MAPLE SYRUP ~ THE FACTS

Maple syrup has been around for hundreds of years, and the basic principle of its production is the same today as it was it the olden times. Sap is collected from maple trees at a specific time of year when the sugar content is high and rendered down to create maple syrup. Modern technology has provided sugar makers with a number of time and labor saving innovations, such as plastic tubing and reverse-osmosis machines, but these inventions do nothing more than hasten the transition from sap to syrup. Real maple syrup is a regional treasure, made more interesting by the fact that it's only possible to produce it in the northern part of North America. Lots of places have sugar maple trees, but there's only one geographical location where weather conditions are such that the trees' sap can be harvested to make authentic maple syrup. Southern Maine lies within the maple syrup production belt, but that said, the window of opportunity to gather the sap, boil it down, and produce maple syrup is usually only six weeks long. The weather dictates how long we have to harvest this unique regional food product.

## HOW DID IT BEGIN?

New Englanders love legends, and legend has it that the first maple syrup maker was a Native American woman from the Iroquois tribe. She was the wife of Chief Woksis. One late-winter morning, the story goes, the chief headed out hunting, but not before yanking his tomahawk from the tree where he'd thrown it the night before. On this particular day the weather turned quite warm, causing the tree's sap to run, leaking from the gash left by the tomahawk and filling a container standing near the trunk. The woman spied the vessel and, thinking it was plain water, cooked the meat for their evening meal in it. The boiling that ensued turned the sap to syrup, flavoring the chief's meal as never before. And thus began the tradition of making maple syrup.

Native Americans converted most of the sap they tapped into sugar, rather than syrup, and used it as an all-purpose seasoning. Salt was not used among the Native American peoples of the northeast. The colonists arrived and the product became known to the settlers as "Indian Sugar", and it became a staple in their diet. Maple sugar was the only form of sweetener in North America until the arrival of the honeybee from Italy in 1630.

Even after the advent of honeybees, honey was scarce and expensive. Molasses and cane sugar became available from the West Indies, but were heavily taxed, and produced with slave labor. Therefore, maple products were not only delicious, but were economically, politically and morally preferable. It's not surprising that just 100 years ago maple products were the sweetener of choice.

## HOW IS IT MADE?

The sap of a maple tree looks like water. It tastes quite a bit like water, too, with just a hint of maple-y sweetness. The particular sap used to make syrup is different from that produced by the tree at any other time of year. This sap flows in the late winter and early spring, when the trees are wakening from their winter's nap and before they start to bud out to produce leaves. Around the time of what the Native Americans called the "sugar moon". After the trees start to bud and produce leaves, the sap changes dramatically, and it has been our experience that the trees simply cease to flow. Some sugar makers experience a "buddy" flavor to their syrup and know that the season has ended for another year.

Three things are required to turn sap into syrup:
● The Trees
Here at High Acres Maple Syrup at Oak Hill Farm, we tap both sugar maples and red maples (also called swamp maples), which, we believe, gives our syrup its very distinctive sweet flavor. The reds start to flow earlier and end their season sooner than the sugars, and we watch them carefully and pull their taps as soon as they are done.
● The Weather
Temperatures during the nights have to be below freezing, preferably in the twenties, with days warming to about 40°F.
● The Equipment
Sugar makers need a way to collect the sap, and a way to boil it down. We collect sap through plastic tubing, boiling it down in

a special evaporator unit. We monitor the boiling sap/syrup for viscosity and sugar density then filter it for clarity, grade it for color and hot-pack it in glass bottles or plastic jugs. (We don't use tin at High Acres Maple Syrup.) The syrup must be over 180°F to prevent mold from growing on the concentrated sugar.

# High Acres Maple Syrup
## South Hiram, Maine

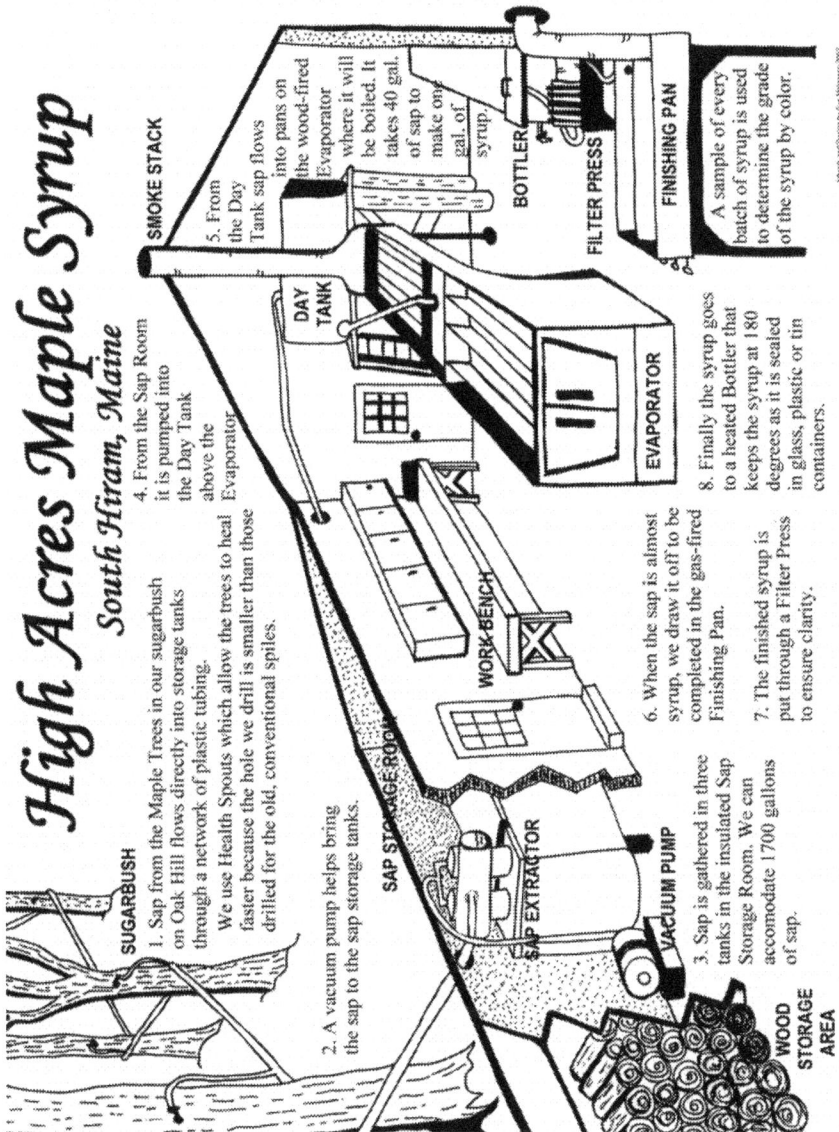

**SUGARBUSH**

1. Sap from the Maple Trees in our sugarbush on Oak Hill flows directly into storage tanks through a network of plastic tubing. We use Health Spouts which allow the trees to heal faster because the hole we drill is smaller than those drilled for the old, conventional spiles.

2. A vacuum pump helps bring the sap to the sap storage tanks.

**SAP STORAGE ROOM**

**VACUUM PUMP**

**SAP EXTRACTOR**

3. Sap is gathered in three tanks in the insulated Sap Storage Room. We can accomodate 1700 gallons of sap.

**WOOD STORAGE AREA**

**SMOKE STACK**

**DAY TANK**

4. From the Sap Room it is pumped into the Day Tank above the Evaporator

5. From the Day Tank sap flows into pans on the wood-fired Evaporator where it will be boiled. It takes 40 gal. of sap to make one gal. of syrup

**WORK BENCH**

**EVAPORATOR**

6. When the sap is almost syrup, we draw it off to be completed in the gas-fired Finishing Pan.

7. The finished syrup is put through a Filter Press to ensure clarity.

**BOTTLER**

**FILTER PRESS**

**FINISHING PAN**

8. Finally the syrup goes to a heated Bottler that keeps the syrup at 180 degrees as it is sealed in glass, plastic or tin containers.

A sample of every batch of syrup is used to determine the grade of the syrup by color.

Artwork and Design by Sue Masterson 2007

## WHAT DO THE GRADES MEAN?

By law, maple syrup is graded strictly by color, not by flavor. In one of our neighboring states the lighter color is favored so much that they charge a premium price for it. The grade will give you an idea about the intensity of the maple flavor in the syrup but taste is a very personal thing, and the flavor will determine what your personal preference will be. Grading systems currently in use in 2007 are:

| US Federal | Vermont | Canadian | Maine |
|---|---|---|---|
| Grade A Light Amber | Fancy Grade | Grade AA | Grade A Light Amber |
| Grade A Medium Amber | Grade A Medium Amber | Grade A | Grade A Medium Amber |
| Grade A Dark Amber | Grade A Dark Amber | Grade B | Grade A Dark Amber |
| Grade B | Grade C | Grade C | Grade A Extra Dark Amber |
| Grade B | Commercial | Grade D | Commercial |

• Light Amber ~ Light and mild, usually made earlier in the season when the weather is colder and there's less chance of sap fermentation – one of the factors that contributes to dark syrup. This has a "maple bouquet," or a very delicate but clear maple flavor. Light Amber is used for making maple candy, maple cream, cake icings, ice cream, and sweets.

• Medium Amber ~ This grade is generally made about midseason, after the weather starts to warm a little. It has a more pronounced maple flavor and is the most popular with the consumer. Medium Amber is used as table syrup on pancakes, waffles, and French toast, as well as an all-purpose syrup for everything from your morning coffee to an indulgence over ice cream.

• Dark Amber ~ This is usually made later in the season as days get longer and warmer. With a deep color and a stronger maple flavor, this is characterized by some as "caramel-like". Its bold flavor works well in baked goods.

• Extra Dark Amber ~ This is our favorite! It is made late in the season and becomes a very dark, intensely flavored syrup. It is most often used for cooking and baking, but here at Oak Hill Farm we prefer its robust maple flavor for everything. Its boldness works well with meat glazes, baked beans, Captain Art's Microwave Acorn Squash and Sue Melanson's Maple Syrup Apple Pie.

• Commercial ~ This grade is a frustration and a quandary for us. It has the strongest maple flavor and tastes wonderful but, because of its color, it cannot be sold in the State of Maine, by law, in less than a one-gallon container. We have visitors ask for this grade continually.

**IS IT ORGANIC?**

Because trees are part of a wild environment, they're inherently, naturally organic. If the forest is responsibly maintained and wisely tapped, there should be no need to enrich the soil. Who would consider fertilizing a mature 100-year-old tree that is obviously thriving in its natural state? Therefore, fertilizer doesn't enter the picture in most maple syrup operations. The same applies to pesticides and herbicides. Many sugar makers, especially the small ones, have never applied for organic certification. We just assume that the public will acknowledge that responsibly produced maple syrup, whether certified organic or not, is an environmentally sound, sustainable product.

**CARE OF YOUR SYRUP**

Unopened maple syrup can be stored on a shelf in a cool place. It can even be stored in the freezer since it will never freeze solid. After it is opened, the refrigerator is the best place to keep it. If it develops sugar crystals, you can warm the syrup to dissolve them. If any surface mold appears, which is extremely unlikely in the fridge, skim the mold off the top, heat the syrup to 200 degrees, wash the bottle out with soap and very hot water, rinse well, dry thoroughly and replace the syrup.

Tin cans can give a metallic taste to syrup. If you've bought canned syrup, decant it into a clean glass jar or bottle. Before returning maple syrup to the refrigerator, rinse the cap in hot water and wipe the top of the jug so the cap will be easier to remove the next time.

## SQUIRRELS

We're not the only creatures who practice sugar maple tapping. The North American squirrel, *Sciurus carolinensusk*, also taps during sugaring season by gouging the bark of young maple trees with their two front teeth and drinking the sap that flows out; if the trickle freezes, they eat the icicles!

## SUBSTITUTING MAPLE SYRUP IN THE KITCHEN

Basically, you have to account for three things when substituting maple syrup for a sweetener in a recipe: the syrup is sweeter than sugar, and it adds extra moisture to the recipe, as well as a slight acidity.

General Cooking. Use three-fourths (75%) the amount of maple syrup as sugar in a recipe. For example, if a recipe says to use 1 cup of sugar, use ¾ cup of maple syrup instead.

Baking. Baking is a little tricky and will depend on the recipe. For every cup of sugar you will want to substitute between ¾ cup (75%) to 1-½ cups (150%) maple syrup, and reduce the dominant liquid in the recipe by 2 to 4 tablespoons. Don't cut back on a liquid that is likely to alter the flavor or texture of a recipe, such as the liqueur, oil, or egg, when you have 2 cups of milk to play with. You may also need to add ¼ to ½ teaspoon baking soda to reduce maple syrup's slight acidity. This will not be necessary in recipes with buttermilk, sour milk, or sour cream.

Substituting for Honey. Honey and maple syrup amounts are equivalent.

Temperature. Maple syrup not only adds a brownish tinge to whatever it is you're cooking, but also tends to make baked goods brown more quickly than sugar does. Reducing the oven temperature by 25°F can compensate for that.

## MAPLE NUTRITION

In addition to tasting great, pure maple syrup offers some nutritional benefits.

Sugar: Sugar is the main nutrient, an important source of energy. Glucose is the sweetest sugar, with fructose next, and sucrose less sweet. The main sugar in pure maple syrup is sucrose. Darker grades have varying amounts of sucrose, fructose, and glucose.

Calories: Maple syrup has about 50 calories per tablespoon.

Vitamins and Minerals: Pure maple syrup has calcium (13.4 mg per tablespoon), potassium (40.8 mg per tablespoon), magnesium, manganese, phosphorus, and iron; trace amounts of B2 (riboflavin), B5 (pantothenic acid), niacin, and folic acid,

Cholesterol: Maple syrup has no cholesterol.

## SYRUP BY THE NUMBERS

Under optimal conditions, it takes 40 gallons of sap, boiled down, to produce 1 gallon of syrup. On a smaller scale, that means it takes 2 gallons of sap to produce 1 cup of syrup. Comparing that to milk, you will need two big gallon milk jugs of sap, to make one school-lunch milk carton of maple syrup.

It takes about one cord of wood or 60 gallons of oil to boil 800 gallons of sap to produce 20 gallons of syrup. Depending on the size of the evaporator used, that would require anywhere from 2 hours to 2 days of boiling.

We have a 4' x 12' wood-fired drop-flue type evaporator manufactured by the Leader Company. It takes us about 7 hours to boil down 800 gallons of sap to make 20 gallons of syrup. We need to have at least 90 gallons of sap in the evaporator to fire it up, but once we get going we are processing the sap from 1000 taps.

Some people wince at the price difference between pure maple syrup and maple flavored pancake syrup, which is generally about 98% to 100% corn syrup. Thinking about what it takes to produce the real thing puts that into perspective, not to mention that the flavor is in no way comparable.

**Maple with Ham Appetizer Biscuits**
• Ingredients
2 cups all-purpose flour
3 teaspoons baking powder
¾ teaspoon salt
¼ cup plus 1 Tablespoon butter
⅔ cup milk
⅓ cup plus 2 Tablespoons High Acres maple syrup
¼ pound smoked ham, very thinly sliced
• Preparation
  Preheat oven to 425°F. Combine flour, baking powder, and salt in a large mixing bowl. Stir with a whisk to blend. Add ¼ cup butter and cut it in until it crumbles. Make a well in the center. Blend together the milk and ⅓ cup maple syrup. Pour into the dry mixture and stir with a fork until the dough holds together. Turn out onto a lightly floured surface and knead 20 to 25 times. Press the dough into a flat 9-inch square. Smooth the surface with a rolling pin. Trim the edges with a floured chef's knife, using a firm downward motion. Cut the dough into 6 strips. Then divide the strips into 6 equal portions to form 36 squares. Transfer to a greased baking sheet. Melt the remaining Tablespoon of butter and stir into the remaining 2 Tablespoons of maple syrup. Brush over the tops of the biscuits. Bake for 12-15 minutes or until nicely browned. Cool on a rack and split with a fork. Place slices of ham between the biscuit halves and serve as an appetizer. Makes 36.

**Maple Cocktail Sausage Spears**
• Ingredients
1 can pineapple chunks in syrup (13-½ oz)
2 packages of brown & serve sausage links (8 oz)
4 Tablespoons cornstarch
⅓ cup water
⅓ cup vinegar
1 medium green pepper cut in ¾ inch squares
½ teaspoon salt
½ cup drained maraschino cherries

½ cup High Acres maple syrup
• Preparation
Drain pineapple, reserving ½ cup liquid. Cut sausages in thirds crosswise and brown in skillet. At serving time, blend cornstarch, salt, reserved liquid, maple syrup, water and vinegar in chafing dish. Heat to boiling over direct heat stirring constantly. Cook and stir a few minutes more. Add drained pineapple, sausage, green pepper chunks and cherries. Heat through. Keep warm over hot water. Spear with cocktail picks. Makes about 150 appetizers.

**Scallops with Bacon & Maple Cream**
• Ingredients
2-½ cups heavy or whipping cream
⅓ cup High Acres maple syrup
1-½ Tablespoons Dijon mustard
½ teaspoon grated nutmeg
Salt and freshly ground white pepper to taste
1-½ pounds fresh bay scallops
1 pound sliced maple-cured bacon
2 Tablespoons snipped fresh chives or minced fresh parsley
• Preparation
Combine the cream and maple syrup in a medium saucepan. Bring just to a boil, and then simmer until reduced almost by half, 15 to 20 minutes. Stir in the mustard, nutmeg, salt and pepper, simmer a few minutes more and remove form the heat. Cut the bacon slices so that they wrap once around the scallops. Wrap each scallop in a piece of bacon. Place the scallops in rows on a broiling tray. (The recipe can be prepared in advance to this point. Refrigerate the sauce and scallops up to eight hours.) When ready to serve, preheat the broiler. Warm the cream sauce over medium-low heat. Broil the scallops four to five inches from the heat until the bacon is browned and crisp, four to five minutes. Transfer the hot scallops with toothpicks to a shallow serving dish that will just hold them in a single layer. Pour the maple cream over all, sprinkle with chives, and serve at once. Makes 8 to 10 appetizer servings.

## CHAPTER 3
## BEEF, FRANKFURTERS and VENISON

**Beef and Eggplant Maple Curry**
• Ingredients
2 Tablespoons olive oil, divided
1-½ pounds stew beef, cut into bite-sized pieces
1 large red onion, chopped medium
1 red or green bell pepper, chopped medium
1 medium eggplant, peeled and cut into ½-inch cubes
1 Tablespoon curry powder
Pinch cayenne pepper, or more, to taste
3 Tablespoons dark High Acres maple syrup
4 Tablespoons soy sauce
Couscous or rice
Garnish: minced fresh parsley
• Preparation
In a large sauté pan, heat 1 Tablespoon of the olive oil over medium-high heat until almost smoking. Add the meat and cook, stirring, until brown all around the edges. Remove with a slotted spoon and set aside. Reduce heat to medium, and add onion and remaining olive oil, and cook, stirring occasionally, until onion is barely translucent, about 5 minutes. Add the curry powder and cayenne pepper, and cook 3 minutes longer. Return the meat to the pan and reduce heat to medium-low. Add the maple syrup and soy sauce, stir thoroughly, cover loosely, and cook, stirring occasionally, 40 minutes, or until sauce is reduced and meat is tender. Serve over rice, garnished with minced fresh parsley. Yield: 6 servings

**Beef Maple Teriyaki Skewers**
• Ingredients
¼ cup High Acres maple syrup
¼ cup soy sauce
2 Tablespoons vegetable oil
2 Tablespoons sesame oil
1 Tablespoon five-spice powder
2 pounds lean beef, sliced across the grain into ¼" strips
• Preparation

Mix the maple syrup, soy sauce, vegetable oil, sesame oil, and five-spice powder in a large non-reactive bowl. Add the beef and toss well to coat the meat. Cover and refrigerate overnight; stir occasionally. Prepare a grill or broiler for medium-high heat. Drain the beef and pat dry with paper towels. Thread the meat onto eight long or sixteen short skewers (if using wooden skewers, soak them in water for 30 minutes before threading on the beef). Grill or broil the beef until tender, turning occasionally, about 6 minutes total for medium rare.

**Corned Beef Braised with Maple**
• Ingredients
4 lbs. corned-beef brisket, desalted
1 cup High Acres maple syrup
Optional ¼ cup bourbon
• Preparation
Place brisket on rack in roasting pan and bake at 325°F uncovered for half an hour. Reduce heat to 275°F, cover, and bake 2 more hours. Uncover, discard all but ½ cup of the liquid that has accumulated in the roasting pan, add maple syrup and bourbon, and continue baking, basting frequently, for 1 hour more. Save liquid as table sauce.

**Frankfurters with Maple Glaze**
• Ingredients
1 pound frankfurters
2 Tablespoons butter, melted
1 Tablespoon soy sauce
1 Tablespoon High Acres maple syrup
• Preparation
Combine butter, soy sauce and maple syrup in frying pan. Score frankfurters or cut them into pieces and add to simmering sauce. Stir until meat is coated and then simmer until sauce is dark and slightly thick. The longer these are heated the better they are. NOTE: These are good both as a main dish and as an appetizer.

**Maple Beef (or Venison) Jerky**
• Ingredients
3 lb. steak cut no more than ¼ inch thick

½ cup soy sauce
2 Tablespoons Liquid Smoke
1 cup Worcestershire Sauce
2 teaspoons Accent
½ teaspoon salt
⅓ cup High Acres maple syrup
1 teaspoon garlic powder
1 teaspoon pepper
• Preparation
Mix ingredients together - marinate 24 hours. Dehydrate about 6 hours, depending on thickness of meat.

## Venison and Mushrooms
• Ingredients
1 lb. Venison (deer meat) pieces
Olive oil
1 cup red wine (Cabernet Sauvignon or Merlot)
2 Tablespoons balsamic vinegar
2 Tablespoons High Acres maple syrup
1 lb. sliced mushrooms
• Preparation
Cook venison pieces in olive oil. Remove meat and add red wine, balsamic vinegar, maple syrup and sliced mushrooms. Cook until sauce thickens and mushrooms are cooked. Add meat to heat through then serve.

*Both Sugar Maples and Red Maples are tapped with Health Spouts that are more tree-friendly than the traditional metal spiles. Sap flows through a network of plastic tubing to sap storage tanks.*

## CHAPTER 4
## BEVERAGES

COLD NON-ALCOHOLIC

### Jamocha Maple Milkshake
- Ingredients
2 Tablespoons High Acres maple syrup
1 teaspoon instant coffee
1 cup milk
½ pint ice cream
- Preparation
Place in blender and blend on high speed until smooth. Makes 2 cups.

### Low-Cal Maple Milk
- Ingredients
1 glass ice-cold milk (preferably 2%)
At least 2 large Tablespoons High Acres maple syrup
- Preparation: Mix together (the mixer adds extra bubbles, which thickens it without adding calories)

### Maple Sesame Milk
- Ingredients
½ cup raw sesame seeds
2 cups milk
3 Tablespoons High Acres maple syrup
1 teaspoon vanilla
- Preparation: Blend until liquid and foamy.

### Rhubarb Maple-Ginger Punch
- Ingredients
6 cups Rhubarb
3 cups water
1 orange
1 lemon
½ cup High Acres maple syrup
¼ cup white sugar
Ginger Ale
- Preparation

Cook rhubarb in a deep heavy saucepan and add water (almost enough to cover rhubarb). You may need a little more or little less. When rhubarb is tender, strain into another bowl. Pour juice back into saucepan. To each quart add juice of 1 orange and 1 lemon. Add maple syrup and sugar to taste. Heat until warm and sugar is dissolved. Chill. When serving, add equal amount of ginger ale.

**Strawberry Cooler**
• Ingredients
8 cups water
6 cups strawberries (hulled, cleaned and chopped)
2 Tablespoons finely chopped orange peel and lemon peel
½ cup High Acres maple syrup
4 cups Ginger Ale
• Preparation
Combine water, strawberries, orange and lemon peel and maple syrup in a pot. Bring to boil. Reduce heat and simmer for 1 hour. Strain through a cheesecloth and refrigerate until chilled. When ready to use, pour about 3 cups of Ginger Ale and slowly add strawberry liquid. Pour into glasses over ice and garnish with a slice of fresh strawberry on a toothpick. Serves 6-8 people.

**Thick Maple Milkshake**
• Ingredients
½ cup High Acres maple syrup
1-½ pints milk
½ pint cream
2 scoops vanilla ice cream
• Preparation
Mix, pour into glasses and serve.

HOT NON-ALCOHOLIC

**Almond Maple Cream for Your Coffee**
• Ingredients
1 cup blanched almonds
1 teaspoon vanilla

¼ cup High Acres maple syrup
¾ water
• Preparation
Blend until smooth and creamy. Great in coffee, but can also be used in place of whipped cream.

## Hot Maple Cider
• Ingredients
6 cups apple cider
¼ cup High Acres maple syrup
Spice bag & string containing:
1 orange peel, cut in strips
1 lemon peel, cut into strips
2 cinnamon sticks
6 whole cloves
6 whole allspice berries
Garnish options:
Cinnamon stick
Thin slice of lemon or orange
• Preparation
Pour cider and syrup into large pot. Place spices and peels in center of a spice bag and tie up with a piece of string. Drop spice bundle into liquid and heat over moderate flame for about 10 minutes. Remove spice bag and discard. Ladle maple cider into mugs and serve warm. Optional: garnish with a stick of cinnamon for stirring, or float thin slice of lemon or orange.

ALCOHOLIC

## Oak Hill Farm Sleigh Ride Cocktail
• Ingredients
Maple sugar, preferably coarse
2 cups store-bought eggnog, chilled
½ cup brandy
½ cup Amaretto liqueur (almond flavor)
1 teaspoon ground nutmeg
2 scoops vanilla ice cream
High Acres maple syrup
• Preparation

Dampen the rims of 4 martini glasses and then line the rims with maple sugar. Combine eggnog, brandy, Amaretto, nutmeg, and ice cream in a blender. Process until smooth. Pour mixture into martini glasses and garnish each glass with a drizzle of High Acres maple syrup.

**Sugarbush Cocktail**
• Ingredients
¾ oz High Acres maple syrup
¾ oz dry gin
1 oz lemon juice
1 oz bourbon
• Preparation
Shake ingredients together and pour over ice.

# CHAPTER 5
# BREADS

YEAST BREADS

## Doug Chapman's Oatmeal Maple Bread
## (A Bread Machine Yeast Bread)
• Ingredients
1 package yeast
1 cup quick cook oatmeal, dry
3 cups bread flour
1 teaspoon salt
⅓ cup High Acres maple syrup
1 Tablespoon cooking oil
1-¼ cups plus 1 Tablespoon very warm water
• Preparation
Put all ingredients into the pan of your Bread Machine according to the directions for your machine. Use the white bread selection. Press start. Yield: 1 loaf

## Maple Rye Yeast Bread
• Ingredients
2 cups hot water
½ cup High Acres maple syrup
2 Tablespoons shortening
1-½ teaspoons salt
1 package yeast
¼ cup warm water
1 cup unsifted rye flour
5-6 cups unsifted all-purpose flour
• Preparation
Mix hot water, maple syrup, shortening and salt until shortening is melted and well blended. Cool. Dissolve yeast in warm water. Add to syrup mixture. Add rye flour and 2 cups unsifted all-purpose flour; beat 4-5 minutes. Add enough flour to make the dough stiff enough to handle. Use remaining flour to cover pastry cloth or board. Knead until dough is smooth and springs back slightly, about 7 to 10 minutes. Dough will be slightly sticky. Place the dough in a greased bowl and turn to grease top. Cover with a damp towel and let rise until double in bulk,

about 2 hours. Punch down and knead lightly on a floured surface. Divide dough into 2 equal portions. Form each into a ball and place in a greased 8" or 9" round cake pan. Cover with a damp towel and let rise about 1 hour. Bake at 350ºF for 45 minutes. Makes two 9" round loaves

## Maple Walnut Pull Apart Bread (A Yeast Bread) (also called Monkey Bread)

- Ingredients

4-½ to 5 cups all-purpose flour
⅓ cup sugar
2 packages of Rapid Rise yeast
1 teaspoon salt
½ cup milk
½ cup water
½ cup butter
2 eggs
1 cup High Acres maple syrup
1 cup chopped walnuts

- Preparation

In a large bowl, combine 2 cups of flour, sugar, undissolved yeast and salt. Heat milk, water and 5 tablespoons butter until very warm (120ºF-130ºF). Stir into dry ingredients. Mix in eggs and enough remaining flour to make soft dough. Knead on floured surface until smooth, about 6 minutes. Cover let rest 10 minutes. Divide dough into 32 pieces; roll into balls. Melt remaining butter. Dip balls in butter. Layer evenly on bottom of greased 10-inch tube or Bundt pan (with non-removable bottom); ⅓ cup maple syrup, ½ cup nuts, 16 balls, ⅓ cup maple syrup, ½ nuts, 16 balls and ⅓ cup maple syrup. Cover and let rise in warm place until it has doubled in size, about 30-40 minutes. Bake in 375ºF preheated oven for 35 minutes or until done. Cover with foil during the last 10 minutes of baking. Invert on serving plate.

QUICK BREADS

## Apricot Pecan Quick Bread

- Ingredients

½ cup packed dried apricots

⅓ cup water
2 cups whole-wheat flour
1 Tablespoon baking powder
¼ teaspoon baking soda
½ cup High Acres maple syrup
2 Tablespoons butter
1 egg
⅓ cup orange liqueur (like Grand Marnier)
¾ cup chopped pecans
• Preparation
Soak apricots for 20 minutes in water. Mix together flour, baking powder, and baking soda. In another bowl, beat maple syrup, butter, and egg. Wring water from apricots into orange liqueur. Stir flour into butter mixture a little at a time, alternating with liqueur mixture. Stir in apricots and nuts. Pour batter into lightly oiled 9"x 5" loaf pan. Bake at 350ºF for 45 to 60 minutes. Bread will be golden brown and toothpick should come out clean when done. Cool before cutting. Makes 1 loaf.

**Easy Maple Walnut Bread (Using Biscuit Mix)**
• Ingredients
½ cup sugar
1 egg
1-¼ cups milk
3 cups prepared biscuit mix (like Bisquick)
1 cup chopped walnuts
½ cup High Acres maple syrup
• Preparation
Several hours before making bread, chop walnuts and add to maple syrup. Let stand, or soak overnight in refrigerator. Preheat oven to 350ºF. Grease two 9"x 5" loaf pans. Combine sugar, egg, milk and biscuit mix. Beat at high speed for 30 seconds. Stir in nut mixture and pour into 2 loaf pans. Bake at 350ºF for 1 hour. Cool before slicing. Yields: 2 loaves.

**Lemon Maple Poppy Seed Quick Bread**
• Ingredients
½ cup milk
⅓ cup poppy seeds
¾ cup High Acres maple syrup

¾ cup butter softened (1-½ sticks)
2 eggs
1 Tablespoon fresh lemon juice
(You can use bottled, but fresh is preferred.)
1 Tablespoon grated lemon peel
1 cup whole wheat flour
1 cup white flour
1-½ teaspoons baking powder
1-½ teaspoons baking soda
½ teaspoon salt
• Preparation
Pre-heat oven to 325ºF. Grease a 9"x 5" loaf pan. Heat the milk to boiling, take off stove, add poppy seeds, and let sit. In a medium bowl beat the maple syrup and butter until smooth. Beat in the eggs and lemon juice and peel. In another bowl, mix all of the dry ingredients. Then, combine all ingredients until smooth, pour into loaf pan and bake for 45 to 50 minutes. Cool on rack for 10 minutes before removing from pan.

## Lemon Maple Zucchini Quick Bread
• Ingredients
3 eggs
1 cup High Acres maple syrup
½ cup vegetable oil
1 teaspoon vanilla extract
Zest of 1 lemon, finely grated
1-½ cups grated zucchini or yellow summer squash
1-½ cups white flour
1 cup whole wheat flour
1 Tablespoon baking powder
½ teaspoon salt
• Preparation
Preheat oven to 350ºF. Grease a 9" by 5" inch loaf pan and set aside. Beat the eggs with an electric mixer for 2 minutes. Gradually add the maple syrup, oil, vanilla, and lemon zest. Stir in the zucchini. Combine the unbleached and wheat flours, baking powder, and salt in a large bowl. Make a well in the center then stir in the zucchini mixture. Blend just until smooth, then turn into the prepared pan. Bake for 50 to 60 minutes, until a tester inserted into the center comes out clean. Cool in the

pan for 5 to 10 minutes, then remove and cool completely on a wire rack.

## Maple Cornbread
• Ingredients
1-⅓ cups sifted all-purpose flour
4 teaspoons baking powder
½ teaspoon salt
⅔ cup cornmeal
⅔ cup milk
⅓ cup High Acres maple syrup
2 eggs, lightly beaten
¼ cup butter, melted
¼ cup High Acres maple syrup
Optional: ½ cup coarsely chopped walnuts, or crumbled bacon
Heat oven to 375°F. Grease 9 inch square cake pan. Sift flour, baking powder and salt into a large mixing bowl. Stir in cornmeal with fork. Combine milk, ⅓ cup maple syrup, butter, and eggs; add to dry ingredients. Stir in just until blended. Spoon into pan and smooth. Drizzle remaining ¼ cup maple syrup over batter. Sprinkle with walnuts and/or bacon. Bake for 25 minutes or until a toothpick comes out clean.

## Maple Date Walnut Quick Bread
• Ingredients
1 cup shredded dates
¾ teaspoon baking soda
1 cup boiling water
1 beaten egg
½ cup High Acres maple syrup
1 teaspoon salt
1 cup flour
1 cup whole wheat flour
1 teaspoon baking powder
½ cup chopped walnuts
• Preparation
Preheat oven to 350ºF. Grease a 9"x 5" loaf pan. Mix together the dates, baking soda, and boiling water. Add the egg and syrup. Mix well. Beat in remaining ingredients. Pour into a greased bread pan and bake for one hour or until done.

## Maple Raisin Quick Bread
• Ingredients
¼ cup butter
¾ cup milk
2 cups flour
½ teaspoon salt
¾ cup High Acres maple syrup
1 egg, well beaten
4 teaspoons baking powder
½ teaspoon baking soda, dissolved in
1 teaspoon hot water
• Preparation
Combine all ingredients in order given. Pour into greased 9"x5"
loaf pan and allow to sit for 20 minutes. Bake 375ºF. for 60
minutes.

## Maple Whole Wheat Quick Bread
• Ingredients
2 cups all-purpose flour
2 teaspoons baking powder
2 teaspoons baking soda
1 teaspoon salt
2 cups whole wheat flour
2 eggs, room temperature
1-½ cups buttermilk, room temperature
½ cup sour cream, room temperature
1-½ cups High Acres maple syrup
• Preparation
In a large bowl, blend together the white flour, baking powder,
baking soda, and salt. Measure and stir in whole wheat flour. In
a small bowl, beat eggs and blend in buttermilk, sour cream
and maple syrup. Pour this liquid mixture into the dry
ingredients and stir well. Grease and line with greased wax
paper, two 9" x 5" loaf pans. Pour or spoon batter into prepared
loaf pans. Cook in a 325ºF oven for 1 hour. Test for doneness.
Turn loaves on their sides and gently tug on the paper to pull
the loaves out. Cool before slicing.

**Orange Maple Walnut Quick Bread**
• Ingredients
2 Tablespoons melted shortening
1 cup High Acres maple syrup
1 egg, well beaten
Rind of one orange, grated
2-½ cups flour
3 teaspoons baking powder
½ teaspoon soda
½ teaspoon salt
¾ cup chopped walnuts
¾ cup orange juice
• Preparation
Grease a 9"x 5" loaf pan. Blend shortening, maple syrup, egg, and orange rind. Sift together flour, baking powder, baking soda, and salt. Add chopped nuts. Add to first mixture alternately with orange juice. Bake in greased pan at 350°F for 1 hour. Bread is better if "ripened" for at least one day before using.

**Pumpkin Cranberry Quick Bread**
• Ingredients
In a small bowl put:
1 cup pumpkin puree
1 egg
1 cup High Acres maple syrup
½ cup vegetable oil
In a large bowl put:
2 cups whole wheat flour, unsifted
¼ teaspoon salt
¼ teaspoon baking soda
1 teaspoon cinnamon
½ teaspoon nutmeg
½ teaspoon cloves
½ teaspoon baking powder
Add small bowl to large bowl, then:
1 teaspoon vanilla
1-½ cups chopped cranberries
• Preparation

Grease a 9"x 5" loaf pan. Bake at 350ºF for 45 minutes. Turn down to 300ºF for 45 minutes more. Cool in bread pan.

**Root Vegetable Quick Bread**
• Ingredients
2 medium Jerusalem artichokes
2 cups whole wheat flour (you can use spelt flour)
1 teaspoon baking soda
1 teaspoon baking powder
1 teaspoon basil (you can use coriander, thyme, sage, or dill)
½ teaspoon salt
1 carrot
½ of a turnip
½ of a parsnip
1 stalk celery
½ cup milk
½ to 1 cup water
2 Tablespoons High Acres maple syrup
• Preparation
Preheat oven to 350ºF. Grease a 9"x 5" loaf pan. Finely chop the artichoke into very small pieces. Place in a bowl with all the dry ingredients. Grate carrot, turnip and parsnip into the mixture. Finely slice celery, and add to the mixture. Add milk, maple syrup, and enough water to moisten the entire mixture. Pour into greased bread pan, and bake for 30 to 35 minutes, or until a skewer pierced through the middle of the bread comes out clean. Remove from the pan, and place on rack to cool. Yield: 1 loaf

MUFFINS

**Maple Apple Muffins**
• Ingredients
2 cups flour, sifted
4 teaspoons baking powder
½ teaspoon salt
1 egg
½ cup milk
½ cup High Acres maple syrup
¼ cup vegetable oil

1-½ cups chopped or diced apples
• Preparation
Sift dry ingredients together into a bowl. Combine egg, slightly beaten with milk, maple syrup, and oil. Add liquid and apples to dry ingredients and mix gently. Spoon into greased muffin tins. Bake at 400° for 18-20 minutes. Makes 12 muffins.

## Maple Walnut Bran Muffins
• Ingredients
¾ cup of wheat bran
1-¼ cups whole wheat flour
3 teaspoons baking powder
½ teaspoon salt
⅓ cup chopped walnuts
½ cup milk
½ cup High Acres maple syrup
1 egg slightly beaten
¼ cup oil
GLAZE
1 Tablespoon butter
1 Tablespoon High Acres maple syrup
½ cup powdered sugar
• Preparation
Combine bran, milk and ½ cup maple syrup in a bowl. Mix in the egg and oil. In a large bowl, combine remaining dry muffin ingredients. Add bran mixture into the dry ingredients, stirring until just moistened. Divide the batter into 12 greased muffin tins. Bake at 400°F oven for 18 to 20 minutes. Glaze: Combine the ingredients, stirring to blend and spread over warm muffins.

## Maple Oatmeal Carrot Muffins
• Ingredients
¼ cup butter
1 egg
¾ cup High Acres maple syrup
1 cup milk
1 cup grated carrots
1 cup oatmeal
1-¼ cups flour
1 Tablespoon baking powder

½ teaspoon salt
½ teaspoon allspice
• Preparation
Beat butter, egg and syrup. Add milk, carrots and oats; blend well. Sift flour, baking powder, salt and allspice. Combine the two mixtures. Fill muffin cups ¾ full with batter. Bake at 400ºF for 20-30 minutes. Yields 12 medium-sized muffins.

## Maple Corn Muffins
• Ingredients
1-⅓ cups flour
⅔ cup cornmeal
3 teaspoons baking powder
⅓ cup High Acres maple syrup
2 eggs
⅔ cup milk
½ teaspoon salt
½ cup melted shortening
• Preparation
Sift dry ingredients together. Beat eggs in bowl; add milk, maple syrup and shortening. Blend dry ingredients in quickly to just moisten flour. Pour into muffin cups and bake at 425ºF for about 20 minutes. Yield: 12 muffins.

## Maple Oatmeal Walnut Muffins
• Ingredients
1-½ cups quick-cooking oatmeal
1 cup all-purpose flour
½ cup light brown sugar
3 teaspoons baking powder
¾ teaspoon salt
½ teaspoon cinnamon
¾ cup milk
1 large egg
¼ cup vegetable oil
¼ cup High Acres maple syrup
½ cup coarsely chopped walnuts
• Preparation
Preheat the oven to 350ºF. Spread the oatmeal on the bottom of a jellyroll pan lined with aluminum foil. Place in the oven for

10 to 15 minutes, or until lightly toasted. Remove and set aside. Increase the oven temperature to 400ºF. Generously grease 12 muffin cups or line with papers. Sift the flour, sugar, baking powder, salt and cinnamon into a large bowl. Whisk to blend thoroughly. Stir in the toasted oats. In a separate bowl, whisk together the milk, egg, vegetable oil, and maple syrup. Make a well in the dry ingredients and pour in the egg mixture. Blend with a wooden spoon until a moist, lumpy batter is formed. Stir in the walnuts. Spoon into the prepared muffin cups and bake for 20 to 25 minutes, or until a wooden toothpick inserted in the center of a muffin comes out clean. Cool on a rack for 5 minutes, then tilt the muffins on their sides or transfer them to the rack to complete cooling. Yield 12 muffins.

## Maple Walnut Yogurt Muffins
• Ingredients
1 cup of white whole wheat flour
1-⅓ cups white flour
½ teaspoon salt
1 teaspoon baking soda
1 teaspoon baking powder
1 egg
⅓ cup High Acres maple syrup
4 Tablespoons oil
1-½ cups plain yogurt
½ cup chopped walnuts
• Preparation
Combined all dry ingredients. Beat together egg, maple syrup, oil and yogurt. Stir in the dry ingredients, just enough to moisten; fold in nuts and spoon into well-greased muffin tins, filling ⅔ full. Bake in 400ºF oven for 15-20 minutes, or until browned.

SCONES

## Frosted Maple Walnut Scones
• Ingredients
SCONES
3-½ cups unbleached all-purpose flour
4 teaspoons baking powder

31

1 teaspoon salt
⅔ cup shortening or butter
1 cup finely chopped walnuts (toast them if you like)
1 cup milk
½ cup High Acres maple syrup
MAPLE FROSTING
1 cup powdered sugar
1 to 2 teaspoons milk
½ teaspoon High Acres maple syrup
• Preparation
In a large bowl, combine the flour, baking powder, and salt. Cut in the shortening and/or butter until the mixture resembles coarse crumbs. Stir in walnuts. In a separate bowl, combine the milk, and maple syrup. Add the wet ingredients to the dry and mix until you've formed a dry soft dough. Flour your work surface generously and scrape the dough out of the mixing bowl onto the floured surface. Divide the dough in half. Gently pat each half of dough into a 7-inch circle about ⅛ inch thick. Transfer dough (it will be soft) onto a lightly greased cookie sheet. This will require two pans. Using a pizza wheel or sharp bench knife, divide each dough circle into eight wedges. Gently separate the wedges so that they're almost touching in the center, but are spaced about an inch apart at the edges. Bake the scones for 15-18 minutes, or until they're golden brown. Combine all frosting ingredients until creamy. Gently frost the tops of scones with the maple frosting. (I let the scones cool slightly before frosting.). Wait a couple of minutes before removing from sheet.

## Maple Pecan Scones
• Ingredients
3 cups flour
1-½ Tablespoons baking powder
¾ teaspoon salt
½ cup butter
2 eggs, beaten
½ cup dark High Acres maple syrup
1 cup chopped pecans
• Preparation

32

Heat the oven to 375°F. Grease and flour a cookie sheet. Combine the flour, baking powder, and salt in a mixing bowl and blend with a whisk. Cut in the butter with a pastry blender or two knives. In a separate bowl beat the eggs; blend in the syrup and cream. Make a well in the center of the dry ingredients and add the wet ingredients all at once. Mix in pecans and stir just enough to blend together. Gather the dough into a ball and roll out between two pieces of waxed paper into a circle about 1-½ inches thick. Cut into 8 pie-shaped pieces and place on the prepared cookie sheet. Brush the tops with additional syrup and bake for 20 minutes. Best served hot.
Yields 8 scones

BISCUITS

**Maple Breakfast Biscuits**
• Ingredients
2 cups flour
1 Tablespoon baking powder
½ teaspoon salt
3 Tablespoons shortening
1-½ cups High Acres maple syrup
• Preparation
Combine dry ingredients. Cut in shortening until it resembles course crumbs. Add milk. Stir just to moisten, and turn onto floured surface. Roll to ½ inch thickness. Cut with a 2 inch biscuit cutter. Pour maple syrup into a 7"x 11" pan, and then place biscuits on top of syrup. Bake at 450ºF for 12 to 15 minutes

ROLLS

**Maple Sticky Rolls (A Yeast Bread)**
• Ingredients Rolls
1 pkg. dry yeast
½ cup hot water
2 cups milk
⅓ cup maple sugar
⅓ cup shortening

1 teaspoon salt
5 to 5-½ cups flour
Butter
High Acres maple sugar
High Acres maple syrup
Cinnamon
• Ingredients Maple Frosting
½ cup butter
2 Tablespoons High Acres maple syrup
2 cups confectioners sugar
3 Tablespoons hot water
• Preparation Rolls
In a large bowl, dissolve yeast in hot water (110ºF to 115ºF). Heat milk, sugar, shortening and salt. When cool, add to the yeast mixture. Stir in flour and knead two minutes until dough is smooth and elastic. Place in greased bowl, cover, and let rise in warm place until doubled in size, about 1 hour. Punch down and divide in half. Roll out ½ inch thick, spread with butter and sprinkle with a mixture of maple syrup, maple sugar and cinnamon. Roll up dough and slice into ¾ inch pieces. Place sliced rolls into pan and let rise 45 minutes. Bake at 350ºF for 30 to 35 minutes. Invert pan to remove. Frost with Maple Frosting.
• Preparation: Maple Frosting
Heat butter until golden brown. Add syrup and sugar and beat, slowly adding hot water until icing spreads smoothly.

**Maple Sticky Rolls (From Frozen Bread Dough)**
• Ingredients
2 loaves frozen bread dough (thawed)
Butter
Cinnamon
1-½ cups cream
1 cup High Acres maple syrup
• Preparation
Roll out 2 loaves frozen bread dough with rolling pin, or one batch homemade roll dough. Spread with butter. Sprinkle with cinnamon and maple sugar. Roll up dough and cut into about 12 pinwheel slices. Set aside. Pour cream and maple syrup into a 9"x 13" cake pan. Stir together. Arrange roll slices in this

mixture, allowing room to rise. Drizzle with maple syrup. When raised, bake at 350ºF until done.

**Maple Glazed Coconut/Walnut Rolls**
**(Using Brown 'n Serve Rolls)**
- Ingredients
¾ cup High Acres maple syrup
⅓ cup butter, melted
⅔ cup sweetened flaked coconut
½ cup chopped walnuts
1 package (1 dozen) brown-n-serve rolls
- Preparation
Preheat oven to 350°F. Combine ½ cup syrup and 2 Tablespoons melted butter and pour into an 8" square pan. Then place pan into oven for 5-8 minutes, or until the syrup-butter mixture bubbles. Sprinkle coconut & nuts over syrup mixture. Combine remaining syrup and butter and dip rolls in mixture, coating on all sides. Arrange rolls upside down on coconut mixture. Return pan to oven and bake 20-25 minutes or until brown. To serve, turn pan upside down on plate.

*Sue fires the evaporator.*

# CHAPTER 6
# BREAKFAST

CEREAL

**Maple Granola**
Combine
½ cup vegetable oil
½ cup High Acres maple syrup
1 teaspoon vanilla
2 cups oatmeal
2 cups Total cereal
1 cup sunflower seeds
¾ cup sesame seeds
½ cup walnuts
½ cup coconut
½ cup wheat germ
1 cup raisins
Spread the all ingredients, except the raisins, on a greased 13"x 9"x 2" pan. Bake at 350°F about 20 minutes. Stir in raisins. Yields about 8 cups.

EGGS

**Baked Eggs in Maple Toast Nests**
• Ingredients
6 Tablespoons butter, plus more for greasing muffin cups
6 Tablespoons High Acres maple syrup
12 slices hearty white bread, crusts removed (I use Pepperidge Farm.)
6 crisp slices smoked Slab bacon
Salt & freshly ground black pepper
Fresh dill
Hollandaise sauce
Paprika
• Preparation
Preheat oven to 400°F. Butter (or spray with Pam) 12 large muffin cups. In a small saucepan, melt butter and add syrup. Flatten bread slices with a rolling pin. Brush both sides with butter/syrup mixture. Carefully form slices into prepared muffin

cups. Be sure bread comes up over edge of muffin cup so eggs won't "escape" over the sides. Crumble bacon and sprinkle it into bottom of each bread-lined cup reserving some for top of each egg. Break an egg into each nest, add salt and pepper to taste and top with remaining bacon. Bake for approximately 15 minutes, or until the eggs are set. Spread warm Hollandaise sauce on individual plates and place a sprig of dill on sauce off to the side. Run a knife around sides of muffin cups to loosen nests and gently lift out, placing two nests on each plate. Sprinkle with paprika, add a tiny piece of dill to the top of each egg and serve immediately.

## Poached Eggs in Maple Syrup
• Ingredients
2 eggs per person
½ cup High Acres maple syrup per person
Croissants (heated) or hot buttered toast
• Preparation
Prepare each serving individually. Put the maple syrup in a small saucepan. Cook until it is very hot. Put the eggs in the syrup and poach until done. Pour over a croissant or hot buttered toast. I put a little bacon or sausage on the side.

FRENCH TOAST

## Blueberry French Toast
• Ingredients
8 slices white bread
(I use dense bread that I make myself or Pepperidge Farm)
2 cups whole milk
8 eggs
1 teaspoon vanilla
¼ cup High Acres maple syrup
8 to 10 blueberries (fresh or frozen) per piece of toast
Butter for cooking
Slightly warm High Acres maple syrup for pouring at the table
• Preparation
Break the eggs in a large baking dish with two-inch sides. Whisk well until whites and yolks are well combined. Add milk, maple syrup and vanilla. Whisk until these ingredients are

combined. Soak the bread in this mix until it is fairly soggy. I put as many slices as will fit on the bottom of the dish and one on top of each or these slices. I then keep turning them over and getting each side to absorb the mix. Put the slices on a buttered medium hot griddle or frying pan. As soon as you place the slices on the cooking surface press the blueberries in the top of each slice of toast. You can be as generous as you like. Cook 5 to 10 minutes on each side. The toast must be firm but not dried out, and browned but not burnt, on each side. Spread a light coat of butter on the cooked toast and serve with maple syrup.

## French Toast with Cream Cheese Stuffing
• Ingredients
¼ cup butter
½ cup High Acres maple syrup
½ loaf bread
(French or raisin preferred, but squishy white bread will do)
4 eggs
1-¼ cups milk
¾ teaspoon vanilla
1 (8 oz.) package of cream cheese
• Preparation
Add butter to saucepan. As it starts to melt, add maple syrup. Cook on medium heat until blended and bubbly. DO NOT bring to a rolling boil. Pour into greased casserole dish. Heat oven to 350°F. Slice bread and make cream cheese sandwiches. Cut into serving size pieces and lay in the casserole dish side by side. Don't overlap. Mix eggs, milk and vanilla with a whisk. Pour over bread, being sure to coat each piece. Bake at 350°F for 40 minutes. Can be prepared the night before and stored in the refrigerator. Top with High Acres maple syrup, whipped cream, or fresh berries.

## Monte Cristo French Toast
Grill French toast as usual, then sandwich Brie cheese and some Smoked Ham or Prosicuitto or Smoked Salmon in between two slices. Continue to cook in the pan until the cheese is slightly melted. Remove and serve with High Acres maple syrup.

# MAKING PANCAKES 101

## Lesson 1: The Batter

*First and foremost, don't beat the batter. When you beat batter you develop the wheat protein (gluten) responsible for the formation of elastic strands. Beating toughens your pancakes. So just stir your liquids into the dry ingredients until they're blended. The best tool is a simple wire whisk or a wooden spoon.*

*Even though pancake recipes always give precise measurements for ingredients, it is quite common for the batter to need adjustment. Generally it needs to be thinned, and this is especially true with whole grains, since they absorb moisture as the batter sits. Most batters are best when they are neither so thin that they run all over nor so thick that you have to spread them around.*

*Give your pancakes extra oomph by adding a tablespoon of maple syrup to the batter before cooking. When a little maple syrup is added to batter mixture, a more even browning will occur.*

*For waffles, simply add more butter to the batter and cook in a waffle iron.*

## Lesson 2: The Cooking Surface

*Basically, the more metal you can put between your heat source and your pancakes, the better. A thick, heavy surface spreads the heat around, and the pancakes cook evenly, whereas a thin pan cooks irregularly and you get "hot spots" on your pancakes. Cast iron is the best especially with low sides, to slide the spatula under the pancakes easily.*

*In our house and in the Barn Kitchen, you will find us using an electric griddle. The advantage of electric is absolute even heat control set at 375°F. We can make six to eight pancakes at a time on our electric griddle.*

*It takes only an initial light rub of oil on your cooking surface to keep pancakes from sticking. After that, the butter in the batter prevents sticking.*

## Lesson 3: Cooking

*Pancakes generally take about 1-½ to 2 minutes to cook on side one, a little less on side two. When little air holes start to show up on the surface and the very edge takes on a dryish* tinge, they're ready to flip. Only flip them once and don't press on them.

Sprinkle berries, nuts, or chocolate chips on top of pancakes just before you flip them.

I have even been known to throw in a kid's chewable vitamin, or kibble for the dog that is allowed to eat from the table. And, indeed, you don't want to mix up the pancake for the Cocker Spaniel and the pancake for the toddler. It's happened!

## Baked Apple Pancakes
• Ingredients
4 eggs
⅔ cup flour
¼ teaspoon salt
⅓ cup milk
¼ cup High Acres maple syrup
3 Tablespoons melted butter
1 Tablespoon salad oil
Filling: 1 (14oz) can apple filling, heated through.
• Preparation
Beat eggs at high speed until fluffy enough to make soft mounds. At low speed beat in small amounts of flour mixed with salt. Alternately add milk mixed with pure maple syrup. Add 2 Tablespoons of melted butter and beat at low speed just until batter is smooth. Combine remaining 1 Tablespoon melted butter with the Tablespoon of oil in heavy ovenproof 10-inch skillet. Pour pancake batter into skillet. Bake in oven at 425°F for 5 minutes. Remove from oven and spoon filling over pancake. Some of the filling will sink into the pancake. Return to oven; reduce heat to 375°F and bake for 12 minutes longer. Serve additional High Acres maple syrup for topping.

## Basic Buttermilk Pancakes
• Ingredients
2 cups all-purpose flour
3 Tablespoons sugar
¾ teaspoon baking soda
1 teaspoon salt

4 Tablespoons (½ stick) unsalted butter, melted, plus extra for cooking
2 large eggs
2 cups buttermilk
½ cup milk
High Acres maple syrup
• Preparation
In a large bowl, whisk dry ingredients together. In a separate bowl, whisk melted butter with eggs until blended, then whisk in buttermilk and milk. Add wet ingredients to dry ingredients, and then stir until just blended. Let batter rest 8 to 10 minutes. Cook on a lightly buttered griddle.

**Cottage Cheese Pancakes**
• Ingredients
2 cups cottage cheese
4 eggs, lightly beaten
4 Tablespoons unsalted butter, melted, plus extra for cooking
1-½ cups all-purpose flour
1 teaspoon baking powder
1 teaspoon salt
1 Tablespoon sugar
• Preparation
Whip cottage cheese in a large bowl until most of the curds are broken up. Add eggs and mix well, then drizzle in butter and whip until smooth. In a separate bowl, stir together flour, baking powder, salt, and sugar. Add wet ingredients to dry ingredients, and then stir until just blended. Cook on a lightly buttered griddle.

**Dutch Bunny Baked Pancake**
• Ingredients
1 cup all-purpose flour
½ teaspoon salt
4 large eggs
1 cup milk
4 Tablespoons (½ stick) unsalted butter
Confectioners' sugar
High Acres maple syrup
• Preparation

Preheat oven to 450ºF. In a medium bowl, sift together flour and salt. In a separate bowl, whisk eggs and milk in a bowl until just combined. Add wet ingredients to dry ingredients, and then stir until just blended. In a heavy 12-inch skillet, melt butter until hot and frothy. Pour batter into skillet and transfer quickly to oven. Bake 20 to 25 minutes, until golden brown and puffed. Do not open oven during baking. Also known as a German Pancake, this has a rich eggy texture and flavor much like popovers. Serve topped with confectioners sugar and High Acres maple syrup.

## Nutty Whole Wheat Cinnamon Pancakes
• Ingredients
¾ cup chopped walnuts, toasted and cooled
⅔ cup whole wheat flour
1-⅓ cups all-purpose flour
1 Tablespoon baking powder
1 teaspoon salt
¼ cup sugar
2-½ teaspoons cinnamon
5 Tablespoons unsalted butter, melted, plus extra for cooking
2 large eggs
2 cups milk
Serve with High Acres maple syrup.
• Preparation
In a food processor, pulse walnuts until they are the texture of cookie crumbs. Set aside. In a large bowl, sift together dry ingredients, and stir in walnuts. In a separate bowl, whisk together butter and eggs, then drizzle in milk and whisk well. Add wet ingredients to dry ingredients, and stir until just blended. Let batter rest 8 to 10 minutes. Cook on lightly buttered griddle.

## Oatmeal Maple Pancakes
• Ingredients
¼ cup High Acres maple syrup
¾ cup milk
1 egg
1 cup pancake mix
½ cup quick cooking oatmeal
2 Tablespoons melted shortening
• Preparation
Combine syrup, milk and egg. Add pancake mix, oats & shortening. Beat lightly until blended. Cook on a lightly buttered griddle.

## Pumpkin Pancakes
• Ingredients
2 cups biscuit mix
2 Tablespoons packed light brown sugar
2 teaspoons ground cinnamon
1-½ cups (12 ounce can) evaporated milk
1 teaspoon ground allspice
½ cup canned pumpkin
2 Tablespoons vegetable oil
2 eggs
1 teaspoon vanilla extract
• Preparation
In large mixer bowl, combine biscuit mix, sugar, cinnamon, and allspice. Add evaporated milk, pumpkin, oil, eggs, and vanilla; beat until smooth. Cook on a lightly buttered griddle.

## Three-Flour Buttermilk Pancakes
• Ingredients
1 cup whole wheat flour
½ cup cornmeal
½ cup unbleached white flour
3 teaspoons baking powder
1 teaspoon salt
2 Tablespoons High Acres maple syrup
3 eggs
2 cups buttermilk
¼ cup oil

• Preparation
Sift flour, baking powder and salt into a large bowl. Separate eggs, adding buttermilk and oil to the yolks. Mix well. Add maple syrup. Beat egg whites until stiff. Slowly add wet ingredients to dry and mix. Try not to over mix, as this will make the pancakes tough. Fold in the egg white and let the batter rest for about 10 minutes. Cook on a lightly buttered griddle.

## Whole Wheat Pancakes
• Ingredients
2 cups whole wheat flour
2 teaspoons melted butter
2 cups water or milk
2 dashes yeast granules
2 eggs
1 teaspoon salt
(Or you can use kelp. I got this from a friend who lives near a seaweed farm in Steuben, Maine. They do use kelp.)
• Preparation
Mix flour, milk or water, and yeast in a bowl, cover and let set overnight. In the morning, add the other ingredients.

TOPPINGS FOR PANCAKES AND WAFFLES

## Apricot Maple Topping
• Ingredients
10 fresh apricots, pitted
1 cup High Acres maple syrup
1 vanilla bean (moist, supple)
• Preparation
Puree 5 apricots in food processor or blender. In small saucepan over medium heat, bring maple syrup to simmer and stir in puree. Slit vanilla bean lengthwise and scrape seeds into syrup mixture. Cut pod into thirds and add to syrup. Continue to simmer 10 minutes, or until syrup thickens slightly. Just before serving, remove bean pod. Thinly slice remaining apricots and add to mixture. Syrup will thicken a little if allowed to cool to room temperature before serving. Keeps in refrigerator 2 weeks. Yield: 2 cups.

**Orange Fig Walnut Topping**
• Ingredients
¼ cup High Acres maple syrup
1 Tablespoon butter
1-½ cups chopped dried figs
½ cup chopped walnuts
½ to ¾ cup water
½ cup orange juice
2 Tablespoons grated orange rind (from 1 large orange)
• Preparation
Heat maple syrup and butter in a small saucepan over moderate heat. Add figs, walnuts, ½ cup water, orange juice, and rind. Heat through and cook, stirring occasionally, 5 minutes until syrupy. Keeps refrigerated 5 to 7 days.

**Maple Applesauce Topping**
• Ingredients
1 cup High Acres maple syrup
1 cup applesauce
• Preparation
Heat maple syrup and applesauce and mix well. Serve warm.

**Maple Cherry Topping**
• Ingredients
1-½ cups High Acres maple syrup
1 cup packed brown sugar
½ cup honey
2 oranges, juiced, retain 1 teaspoon peel
2 lemons, juiced, retain 1 teaspoon peel
2 Tablespoons butter
1 teaspoon ground cinnamon
1 cup dried tart cherries, chopped
• Preparation
Combine maple syrup, brown sugar, honey, juices and grated rind in medium saucepan. Bring to a boil, stirring constantly. Reduce heat, and simmer 10 minutes. Add cherries, and cook 2 minutes. Yield: about 2 cups

## Maple Peanut Butter Topping
• Ingredients
1 cup High Acres maple syrup
¼ cup smooth peanut butter
• Preparation
Gradually beat maple syrup into peanut butter. Beat thoroughly until smooth.

## Pineapple-Ginger Topping
• Ingredients
2 Tablespoons butter
¼ cup High Acres maple syrup
2-½ cups fresh pineapple, chopped medium
2 teaspoons fresh grated ginger
¼ teaspoon cinnamon
• Preparation
Melt butter in a cast-iron skillet over moderate heat. Add maple syrup and pineapple. Stir, and then add ginger and cinnamon. Heat until bubbling, then reduce heat and simmer 10 minutes.

## Whipped Maple Mascarpone
• Ingredients
¾ cup mascarpone cheese
¾ cup heavy cream
3 Tablespoons High Acres maple syrup
1-½ teaspoons vanilla extract
• Preparation
Whip together mascarpone, heavy cream, maple syrup, and vanilla extract at high speed until peaks form. Serve on top of pancakes with extra syrup or with your favorite jam.

WAFFLES

## Buttermilk Waffles
• Ingredients
2 egg whites separated
2 cups buttermilk
2 cups all-purpose flour
2 teaspoons baking powder
1 teaspoon baking soda

½ teaspoon salt
¼ cup plus 2 Tablespoons shortening
2 Tablespoons High Acres maple syrup
• Preparation
Heat waffle iron. Beat egg yolks and remaining ingredients with rotary beater until smooth. Beat egg whites until stiff and fold in. Let rest for 3-4 minutes. Pour batter from cup or pitcher onto center of hot, oiled waffle iron. Bake for about 5 minutes or until steaming stops. Remove waffle carefully.

## YOGURT

**Homemade Flavored Yogurt**
• Ingredients: 1 quart whole milk
⅓ cup maple syrup
⅓ cup instant nonfat dry milk (produces a thicker texture)
1 rounded Tablespoon plain yogurt
Flavorings or fruit (see preparation)
• Preparation
Scald 1 quart of milk and stir in ⅓ cup maple syrup. If other flavors are desired, stir in 1 Tablespoon of extract (such as vanilla, lemon, almond, or peppermint) or instant coffee. Another time, try adding 1 teaspoon of ground spices (cinnamon, nutmeg, mace, ginger, or your own special combination). Add the instant nonfat dry milk, cool the mixture to 110°F, and stir in the culture. Pour into warm containers, cover, and incubate. For jam, preserve and peanut butter flavors, put 1 Tablespoon of the flavoring into the bottom of 1 cup containers and pour the warm milk-yogurt mixture over. Cover and incubate as usual. If fresh, canned, or dried fruit is desired, it is best to make such additions to the yogurt after it has incubated. The acid content of some fruits can curdle the milk-yogurt mixture and prevent proper fermentation. Whenever you are flavoring yogurt, always remember to leave 1 cup plain, so that you will have fresh starter for the next batch.

**Maple Pecan Divinity**
• Ingredients
2 cups High Acres maple syrup
2 egg whites
¼ teaspoon salt
1 teaspoon vanilla
½ cup pecans, broken
• Preparation
Butter the sides of a heavy 2-quart saucepan, then cook the maple syrup rapidly over high heat to hardball stage (250°F.) without stirring. Remove from heat. At once beat egg whites with salt to stiff peaks. Add hot syrup to egg whites and beat at high speed with an electric beater. Continue beating until mixture forms soft peaks and begins to lose its gloss. Stir in the vanilla. Quickly add the pecans. Drop mixture by teaspoonful on waxed paper, swirling each candy to a peak.

**Maple Pralines**
• Ingredients
2 cups sugar
⅔ cup milk
1 cup High Acres maple syrup
2 cups pecan meats
• Preparation
Boil sugar, milk and maple syrup until the mixture reaches the softball stage, or 236°F. Remove from heat, and cool; beat until it is smooth and creamy. Add pecans and drop on buttered paper from the tip of a spoon, making small mounds.

**Maple Sugar Candy**
• Ingredients
2 cups Grade A Light Amber High Acres maple syrup
(Will make about 1 lb. of candy.)
A few drops of vegetable oil or butter
Additional Grade A Light Amber High Acres maple syrup if you are going to do a crystalline coating.
• Equipment

A deep cooking pan (at least 4 cups).
Candy thermometer capable of measuring to 240°F.
Stainless steel mixing bowl & heavy duty mixer.
Double boiler.
Candy molds.
(I use rubber molds, but you can use metal or wooden molds. Small aluminum pans can be used as molds. Hard plastic molds are not for this kind of candy.)
Drying racks (cake cooling racks).
Pot with a basket (like a Fry Daddy).
Waxed Paper.

• Preparation

Pour 1 cup of the maple syrup into a deep 4-cup pan and insert a candy thermometer capable of reading to 240°F. Cook, watching carefully to be sure it does not boil over, until it reaches 240°F. Pour into a stainless steel mixing bowl and quickly cool to a maximum of 100°F. Do not stir or disturb the syrup while it is cooling. When it reaches 100°F stir with the mixer until it lightens in color and the surface looks dull. This is the fondant. Set it aside.

Take the second cup of maple syrup and cook it until it reaches 240°F. While it is cooking place a double boiler on the stove and heat the water in it until it comes to a boil, then shut it off. When the second cup of maple syrup reaches 240°F, pour it into the top of the double boiler and quickly place the fondant into that syrup. Stir briefly just until mixed and pour into molds quickly. Let harden about 15 minutes, take the candy out of the molds and place ion a drying rack for 4 to 18 hours. You then have the option of adding a crystalline coating, which will extend shelf-line. If you are going to gobble up the candy immediately, there is no reason for the next step.

During the time the candy is drying, cook some light amber maple syrup in a pot with a basket that fits into it. (I use a Fry Daddy dedicated just for this purpose.) Cook it until it is 2° to 4° above maple syrup. Place a piece of wax paper on the surface and cool the syrup to room temperature.

When the candy has dried for at least 4 hours minimum, take the wax paper off the syrup and put the candy loosely into the basket. Immerse the basket in the syrup. Cover the surface with fresh waxed paper. Let the candy sit in the coating syrup for 4 to 6 hours, checking now and then until the candy feels like it has sandpaper ion the surface. Remove the candy and drain well, place on racks to dry and turn over several times to keep the candy from sticking to the rack.

**Baked Maple Popcorn**
• Ingredients
½ cup High Acres maple syrup
1 cup butter
2 cups packed maple sugar
1 teaspoon salt
½ teaspoon baking soda
1 teaspoon vanilla extract
1 cup un-popped corn
• Preparation
Pop the popcorn. Put popped corn in a slightly buttered bowl. Heat oven to 250ºF. In a saucepan, melt butter add maple syrup, maple sugar and salt. Boil without stirring for 5 minutes. Remove from heat. Stir in baking soda and vanilla extract. Pour gradually over popped corn and mix well. Turn into large roasting pan; bake 1 hour, stirring every 15 minutes. Remove from oven and cool.

**Maple Fudge**
• Ingredients
2 cups granulated sugar
1 cup High Acres maple syrup, preferably Light Amber
½ cup light cream
2 Tablespoons butter
• Preparation
Grease well an 8-inch-square pan. Combine all ingredients in a medium saucepan. Cook, stirring over medium-high heat, until boiling and continue cooking and stirring until the mixture reaches 238ºF, about 10 to 15 minutes. Remove from heat and cool without stirring until lukewarm (110ºF), about 1 hour. Remove the candy thermometer and beat the mixture with a wooden spoon until the color lightens, the mixture loses its gloss, and the fudge begins to set. Quickly press into the prepared pan; score into squares while warm. When the fudge is firm, cut into squares. Store tightly covered.

## Maple Lollipops

● Ingredients

2 cups High Acres maple syrup (can use any grade but light amber preferred)

⅔ cup glucose, or ⅔ cup corn syrup

Cooking spray like PAM

● Preparation

Select a cloudy colored hard plastic lollipop mold (the clear molds are for chocolate). You will be able to fill 17–35 cavities with this amount. Spray the molds with a cooking spray like PAM. Cook syrup on the stove, and use a high-sided pot with a spout. It will foam but do not use de-foamer. Don't stir like fudge. Heat to 280ºF degrees F. Then just pour into molds, working fast. Put the sticks in the molds and twirl to coat on both sides. Cool 20 minutes. Unmold. Don't bag hot. Use cellophane bags. Humidity can make them limp, especially in summer.

## Maple Nut Brittle

● Ingredients

3 cups High Acres light amber maple syrup

3 Tablespoons butter

1 teaspoon baking soda

Nuts (pecans, peanuts, cashews, walnuts) enough to cover a 13" by 18" shallow pan.

● Preparation

Butter pan well. Spread nuts out on the pan generously. I put them touching each other but not layered. Roast nuts at 325ºF for no more than 10 minutes. Melt butter. Boil syrup to 300º, sift in the baking soda and quickly pour in melted butter, spreading it around as you pour. Stir only very slightly, but with a sharp, whipping action. Then pour quickly over the nuts. Allow to cool, then break into irregular pieces.

## Maple On Snow "Leather Aprons"

Heat the desired amount of syrup to approximately 242ºF (25-30ºF above the boiling point of water). Without stirring, pour immediately onto snow in long stripes. Serve with plastic forks to wind the "Leather Aprons" on. Use of clean, natural snow is customary but out-of-season shaved ice will work to pour the syrup on. A gallon will generally serve about 60 people.

## Pumpkin Candy

• Ingredients

1 quart of pumpkin meat; fresh cut into 1" x 1-½"pieces

2-½ cups water

1 cup High Acres maple sugar or brown sugar

1 cup High Acres granulated white sugar

• Preparation

Place the cubed pumpkin in a saucepan and cover it with water, about 2 to 2-½ cups. Bring it to a boil and simmer for 15 to 20 minutes, uncovered, until the pumpkin is just tender. Remove the pumpkin with a slotted spoon. There should be about 1-½ cups of liquid remaining. Add the sugar and dissolve over low heat. Place the pumpkin pieces back in the pan and bring slowly back to a boil, then lower the heat and simmer for 15 minutes. Let the pumpkin pieces stand in the syrup overnight. The next day, bring the mixture back to a boil and simmer for 5 minutes. Remove the pumpkin pieces from the syrup and spread them out on a wire rack so the pieces are not touching one another. Let them stand in a warm place or in a 140°F oven for 3 to 4 hours to dry. Roll each piece in the maple sugar, and store them in a dry, cool place. Do not stack or crowd the candy together. Note: This can also be made with acorn squash, but the pumpkin gives the candy a more vivid color. The flavor is about the same. Yield: 2 pounds

# CHAPTER 8
# DESSERTS

BARS, COOKIES AND OTHER GOOD THINGS
THAT FIT IN YOUR POCKET

## Chewy Maple Coconut Cookies Like Gramma Made
• Ingredients
1-½ cups all-purpose flour
2 teaspoons baking powder
½ teaspoon salt
½ cup shortening
1 cup packed brown sugar
1 egg
½ cup High Acres maple syrup
½ teaspoon vanilla extract
1 cup flaked coconut
• Preparation
Preheat oven to 375ºF. Lightly grease baking sheets. In medium bowl, combine flour, baking powder and salt. Set aside. In a mixing bowl, cream shortening and brown sugar until fluffy. Beat in the egg, syrup, and vanilla until well mixed. Stir in flour mixture until just mixed and then stir in coconut. Drop mixture by Tablespoonfuls 2 inches apart onto prepared greased baking sheets. Bake for 10 to 12 minutes, or until golden brown. Transfer to wire racks to cool. Store in airtight container.

## Cinnamon Maple Ring Cookies
Pastry
2 cups flour
¼ cup maple sugar
1 cup High Acres maple syrup, chilled
2 to 4 Tablespoons ice water
Filling
¼ cup maple sugar
4 teaspoons ground cinnamon
Topping
¼ cup High Acres maple syrup

Combine flour and sugar. Add butter and mix until the dough forms small, pea-sized pellets. Add chilled maple syrup and 2 Tablespoons water, and mix. Do not over mix. Separate dough into 2 balls and flatten into disks. Wrap dough tightly in plastic wrap. Refrigerate 2 hours until firm. To prepare the filling: combine sugar and cinnamon in bowl. Roll one piece of dough into a rectangle 10"wide, 15" long, ⅛" thick. Prepare by sprinkling filling, rolling and sealing edge by pressing after moistening with water. Repeat for 2nd roll. Refrigerate 1 hour. Using a sharp knife, cut ¼" slices from each roll. Place slices on ungreased baking sheets 1" apart. Brush tops lightly with ¼ cup maple syrup. Bake at 325° for 16-17 minutes. After baking, immediately transfer to a flat surface with a spatula to cool.

## Easy Maple Walnut Squares
• Ingredients
3 beaten eggs
½ teaspoon salt
⅔ cup cooking oil
¾ cup chocolate chips
1 cup High Acres extra dark maple syrup
½ cup chopped walnuts
1 teaspoon vanilla
2 cups flour
1 teaspoon baking powder
• Preparation
Mix in order given. Pour into 9"x 13" pan and bake at 350ºF for 30 minutes. Do not over bake

## Maple Walnut Coconut Bars
• Ingredients
½ cup sugar
1 egg
⅔ cup flour
1 cup rolled oats
1 teaspoon vanilla
½ cup soft shortening
½ cup High Acres maple syrup
1 cup chopped nuts
½ teaspoon baking powder

½ cup coconut

• Preparation

Mix all of the ingredients thoroughly. Spread in 8"x 8" square greased pan. Bake 350ºF for 30-35 minutes. While warm, cut in squares.

## Maple Cookie Rollups

• Ingredients

½ cup High Acres maple syrup

¼ cup butter

½ cup sifted flour

¼ teaspoon salt

Whipped cream

Chopped walnuts

• Preparation

Preheat oven to 350ºF. Bring maple syrup and butter to a hard boil for ½ minute. Remove from heat; add flour and salt. Stir in well. When blended, drop 1 Tablespoon dough onto greased cookie sheet three inches apart. Bake 9 to 12 minutes or until the color of maple sugar. Remove pan from oven. When slightly cooled, remove cookies with spatula. Roll like a crepe, and cool on a rack. Fill with whipped cream and dip ends in chopped nuts at serving time.

## Maple Fruit Meringues

• Ingredients

1 cup High Acres maple syrup

2 egg whites

⅓ cup seedless raisins

⅓ cup candied lemon peel

⅓ cup chopped figs (optional)

1 cup broken nutmeats

• Preparation

Measure maple syrup into large saucepan. Boil to 254ºF, when syrup forms a firm ball when dropped in cold (not ice) water. Meanwhile, beat egg whites until stiff, but not dry. Add hot syrup gradually, beating constantly. Continue beating until mixture stands in firm peaks. Fold in raisins, lemon peel, figs and nuts. Drop by teaspoonfuls (about 1" apart) on lightly greased baking sheet and bake in 200ºF oven one hour.

## Maple Hermits
• Ingredients
1 cup soft shortening
2 cups High Acres maple syrup
4 eggs
¼ cup strong coffee
2 cups seedless raisins
1 cup chopped nuts
4 cups flour
1 teaspoon salt
1 teaspoon baking soda
1-½ teaspoons nutmeg
• Preparation
Heat oven to 375ºF. Combine shortening, syrup and eggs. Beat until fluffy. Stir in coffee, raisins and nuts. Sift flour, salt, soda and nutmeg together into first mixture and stir to blend. Drop by rounded teaspoonful on greased cookie sheets. Bake 10 to 12 minutes or until set.

## Maple Pecan Squares
• Ingredients
CRUST
1-½ cups flour
¼ cup brown sugar
½ cup butter
FILLING
½ teaspoon vanilla
1 cup High Acres maple syrup
2 eggs beaten
2 Tablespoons flour
¼ teaspoon salt
⅔ cup brown sugar
1 cup chopped pecans
• Preparation
Combine flour, ¼ cup brown sugar and butter. Mix with fork until consistency of corn meal. Press into a 9"x 13" pan and bake 15 min. at 350ºF. Combine ⅔ cup brown sugar and maple syrup in small saucepan and simmer for 5 minutes. Pour over beaten eggs slowly, stirring constantly. Stir in remaining ingredients except nuts. Pour mixture over baked crust.

Sprinkle with nuts and bake at 350ºF for 20 to 30 minutes. Cool in pan. Cut into bars.

**Maple Pumpkin Apple Cookies**
• Ingredients
1 cup High Acres maple syrup
1 cup pumpkin puree, canned or fresh cooked and cool
1 egg
1 teaspoon vanilla extract
½ cup unsalted butter
1 cup flour
1 cup whole wheat flour
1 teaspoon baking soda
1 teaspoon baking powder
½ teaspoon salt
½ teaspoon cinnamon
½ teaspoon nutmeg
½ cup chopped pecans
1 cup peeled grated apples
• Preparation
Preheat oven to 350ºF. Combine the maple syrup, pumpkin puree, egg and vanilla in a blender or food processor and process until smooth. Cream the butter with an electric mixer, then stir in about half the blended mixture. In a separate bowl, toss together the flours, baking soda, baking powder, salt, and spices. Add half of this to the creamed mixture, stirring just until blended. Stir in the rest of the pumpkin puree, followed by the remaining dry mix. Gently fold in the pecans and apple. Spoon heaping tablespoons of the batter onto a greased baking sheet, leaving a couple of inches between them for spreading. Bake for 15 to 20 minutes, until the bottom edges just start to brown. Transfer to racks and cool. You may also substitute winter squash for the pumpkin.

**Maple Sugar Cookies**
• Ingredients
1 cup butter
1 cup white sugar
¾ cup High Acres maple syrup
2 eggs, well beaten

2 teaspoons milk
2 teaspoons vanilla
4 cups flour
2 teaspoons baking soda
½ teaspoon salt
• Preparation
Cream together the butter, sugar and syrup. Add eggs, milk and vanilla. Add flour, baking soda and salt (sifted together). Mix all thoroughly. Chill dough well then roll out thin on floured board and cut with cookie cutter. Drop by teaspoonfuls onto greased pan. Flatten with glass dusted with sugar. Bake on greased cookie sheet at 350ºF for 10 minutes.

## Oatmeal Raisin Walnut Cookies
• Ingredients
½ cup butter
1 cup High Acres maple syrup
1 beaten egg
1-½ cups flour
1 teaspoon salt
2 teaspoons baking soda
¼ cup milk
1-½ cups oatmeal
½ cup raisins
½ cup chopped walnuts
• Preparation
Preheat oven to 375ºF. Beat butter, maple syrup and egg together until fluffy. Stir flour, salt and baking soda together. Add to first mixture. Add milk and oatmeal. Mix well. Stir in raisins and nuts. Drop by spoonfuls on a greased cookie sheet. Bake for 15 minutes or until done.

## Soft Almond Maple Cookies
• Ingredients
⅓ cup unsalted butter, at room temperature
3 ounces cream cheese at room temperature
¾ cup High Acres maple syrup, at room temperature
1 egg
1 teaspoon almond extract
2 teaspoons finely grated lemon zest

2 cups almond meal
1-½ cups flour
½ teaspoon salt
1 teaspoon baking powder
• Preparation
Preheat the oven to 350ºF. Using an electric mixer, cream the butter and cream cheese. Continue to beat, adding the maple syrup in a slow drizzle. Next, beat in the egg, almond extract, and lemon zest. Toss together the remaining ingredients, and then add them to the creamed mixture, stirring just until everything is blended. Spoon Tablespoonfuls of dough onto a lightly greased baking sheet, leaving just a little room between them. Bake, only one sheet at a time, for about 15 minutes, until the bottoms are golden and the tops just slightly resistant to light pressure. Transfer the baked cookies to a rack to cool.

## Streusel Pecan Squares
## (Gramma's version of Maple Pecan Squares)
• Ingredients
CRUST
3 cups flour
¾ cup brown sugar
1-½ cups butter
• Preparation
CRUST
Preheat oven to 400ºF. Lightly spoon flour into measuring cup, level off. In large bowl, combine all crust ingredients at low speed until crumbly. Reserve 2 cups crumb mixture for filling and topping. Press the remaining crumb mixture into bottom and ¾" up the sides of an ungreased 15"x 10"x 1" baking pan. Bake at 400ºF for 10 minutes.
• Ingredients
FILLING
¾ cup brown sugar
1-½ cups High Acres maple syrup
1 cup milk
⅓ cup butter
1 teaspoon vanilla
4 eggs
1-½ cups pecans

- Preparation
FILLING
In large bowl, combine ¼ cup reserved crumb mixture and all filling ingredients except pecans. Pour over prebaked crust; bake an additional 10 minutes. Reduce oven temperature to 350ºF. Sprinkle remaining 1-¾ cups reserved crumb mixture over filling; bake at 350ºF for 20-25 minutes until filling is set and crumb topping is golden brown. Serve with whipped cream or ice cream, if desired.

## CAKES and COFFEE CAKES

### Ball Cakes in Maple Syrup
- Ingredients
1 quart water
1-¼ cups + 1 Tablespoon brown sugar
1-¼ cups + 1 Tablespoon High Acres maple syrup
1-¼ cups + 1 Tablespoon flour
2 teaspoons baking soda
2 Tablespoons sugar
1 teaspoon salt
3 eggs
½ cup + 1 teaspoon butter, cut into ½" cubes
1 cup + 1 Tablespoon + 1 teaspoon 2% milk
- Preparation
In large pan, stir water and brown sugar and let simmer until sugar is completely dissolved. Then add maple syrup and let it simmer, again. Prepare the cakes: mix in a metal or plastic bowl, flour, baking soda, sugar and salt. Add eggs, butter and milk gradually. Mix together, delicately and set aside. Bring the sauce to boil. Form the ball cakes by hand and add to the boiling sauce with a large spoon. Cover and let simmer for 20-25 minutes. Serve very hot with vanilla ice cream.

### Maple Ginger Cake
- Ingredients
½ cup white sugar
2 Tablespoons shortening
1 egg (well beaten)
1 Tablespoon baking soda

60

½ teaspoon salt
¼ cup molasses
¼ cup High Acres maple syrup
½ cup buttermilk
1 teaspoon ginger
1-½ cups flour
• Preparation
Mix ingredients in order as given, beat well, bake in moderate oven, 350ºF for 35-40 minutes. This makes a delicious dessert to serve with whipped cream or served with vanilla ice cream with High Acres maple syrup poured over it.

## Maple Glazed Pumpkin Ring
• Ingredients Pumpkin Ring
1-½ cups all-purpose flour
1 teaspoon baking soda
1 teaspoon cinnamon
¼ teaspoon ground allspice
¼ teaspoon salt
½ cup unsalted butter; softened
¾ cup packed light brown sugar
2 large eggs
1 cup solid-pack canned pumpkin
⅓ cup maple syrup
1 teaspoon pure vanilla extract
• Ingredients Glaze
1 cup confectioners' sugar
2 Tablespoon sour cream
1 Tablespoon High Acres maple syrup
1 Tablespoon fresh lemon juice
• Preparation
Heat oven to 350ºF. Grease a 6-½ cup capacity ring mold. Sift together flour, baking soda, cinnamon, allspice and salt; set aside. Beat butter and brown sugar with an electric mixer until light. Add eggs, one at a time, mixing well after each addition. Stop mixer and add pumpkin, syrup and vanilla. Mix in on low speed. Add dry ingredients and fold in with a rubber spatula. Transfer batter to prepared pan. Bake until a toothpick inserted in the center comes out clean, 30 to 35 minutes. Cool in pan 5 minutes then carefully loosen from sides of pan with a small

61

knife Invert onto a wire rack placed over a sheet of waxed paper. Meanwhile, prepare glaze. Sift confectioners' sugar into a medium bowl. Add remaining ingredients and mix until smooth, then spoon over warm cake letting the glaze drip down sides. Cool completely.

## Maple Hazelnut Coffee Cake
• Ingredients
1-½ cups all-purpose flour
⅔ cup packed light brown sugar
¼ cup chopped hazelnuts
3 Tablespoons frozen apple juice concentrate
1 Tablespoon vegetable oil
½ teaspoon ground cinnamon
¼ teaspoon salt
¼ cup High Acres maple syrup, preferably dark grade.
CAKE
2 cups all-purpose flour
1-¼ teaspoons baking powder
¾ teaspoon baking soda
1 teaspoon salt
1 large egg
1 large egg white
⅔ cup packed light brown sugar
¾ cup nonfat plain yogurt
⅓ cup applesauce
¼ cup High Acres maple syrup, preferably dark grade
2 Tablespoons oil
1 teaspoon vanilla extract
Confectioners' sugar for dusting
TO MAKE CRUMB TOPPING:
In a food processor, combine flour, brown sugar, hazelnuts, apple juice concentrate, oil, cinnamon and salt. Pulse until crumbly. Add maple syrup and pulse until combined. Set aside.
TO MAKE CAKE:
Preheat oven to 325ºF. Lightly oil and 8"x 11½" inch baking dish or coat it with nonstick spray. In a bowl, combine flour, baking powder, baking soda and salt. In a medium bowl, whisk egg, egg white and brown sugar until smooth. Add yogurt, applesauce, maple syrup, oil and vanilla; whisk until smooth.

With a rubber spatula, fold fry ingredients into wet ingredients until just combined. Do not over mix. Scrape batter into prepared pan and sprinkle evenly with crumb topping. Bake cake for 45 to 50 minutes, or until a skewer inserted in the center comes out clean. Let cool almost completely. Dust with confectioners' sugar. Serve warm or at room temperature.

## Maple Lemon Pineapple Cake (from a mix)
• Ingredients
1 lemon cake mix (white cake is fine too)
(19 oz) can unsweetened crushed pineapple
¼ cup High Acres maple syrup
Mix these two ingredients together and set aside.
(8 oz) Cream Cheese
1-½ cups milk
1 Tablespoon High Acres maple syrup
1 package lemon or vanilla instant pudding
Cool Whip
High Acres maple syrup for drizzle
• Preparation
Mix cake mix and bake as directed on box using a 9"x13" inch pan. When the cake is baked and removed from the oven spread the pineapple and ¼ cup of Maple Syrup over the cake. Let cool for at least on hour. Beat cream cheese in medium size bowl and blend in milk, maple syrup, and pudding until real smooth. Spread over cake and refrigerate until ready to serve. Top with Cool Whip and drizzle Maple Syrup over each serving. This cake can be made the day before.

## Maple Pumpkin Cake
• Ingredients
¼ cup butter, melted
1-¼ cups graham cracker crumbs
¼ cup sugar
3 each (8 oz) packages cream cheese, softened
1 each (14 oz) can of sweetened condensed milk (not evaporated milk)
1 cup High Acres maple syrup
1 (16 oz) can of pumpkin
3 eggs

1-½ teaspoons ground cinnamon
1 teaspoon ground nutmeg
½ teaspoon salt
● Preparation
Combine butter, crumbs and sugar. Press into 9" spring-form pan. In large mixing bowl, beat cheese until fluffy. Gradually beat in sweetened condensed milk until smooth. Add ¼ cup syrup and remaining ingredients. Pour into prepared pan. Bake at 300ºF oven for 1 hour and 15 minutes or until set, (center will be slightly soft). Cool and then chill. Top with MAPLE PECAN GLAZE, as follows. In saucepan, combine remaining ¾ cup maple syrup and 1 cup of whipping cream. Bring to a boil. Boil rapidly 15 to 20 minutes, stirring occasionally. Cool. Add ½ cup chopped pecans.

## Maple Spice Cake
● Ingredients
1-½ cups sifted flour
2 teaspoons baking powder
½ teaspoon salt
½ teaspoon cinnamon
⅛ teaspoon ground ginger
¼ cup butter
1 cup High Acres maple syrup
1 cup apple sauce
2 eggs, beaten
⅓ cup milk
¼ teaspoon nutmeg
● Preparation
Sift together dry ingredients into a large mixing bowl. Set aside. In a separate bowl combine remaining ingredients. Sift dry ingredients gradually into liquid mixture. Blend well. Pour batter into a 9-inch square greased pan. Bake in preheated 350ºF oven for 40-50 minutes. Frost with maple frosting. (FROSTING page 72)

## Maple Sponge Cake
● Ingredients
¾ cup High Acres maple syrup
4 eggs, separated

¼ teaspoon salt
½ teaspoon vanilla
1 cup sifted flour
½ teaspoon baking powder
• Preparation
Heat syrup to boiling point; slowly pour on the beaten egg whites, beating constantly. Fold in beaten egg yolks, vanilla, salt, flour and baking powder. Bake in tube pan at 325ºF for 50 minutes.

## Old-Time Maple Gingerbread
• Ingredients
½ cup High Acres maple syrup
2 cups flour
½ teaspoon salt
1 teaspoon ginger
1 teaspoon baking soda
2 eggs
1 cup sour cream
• Preparation
Preheat oven to 325ºF. Combine and sift dry ingredients. Mix maple syrup with beaten eggs and add sour cream. Combine the mixture and bake in greased 8" x 8" pan for 20 to 30 minutes. Serve warm.

## Sugarhouse Sugar-On-Snow Cake
(Walnut Cake with Maple Meringue Frosting)
• Ingredients
CAKE
¾ cup walnuts
1-½ cups flour
2 teaspoons baking powder
1 teaspoon baking soda
½ teaspoon salt
1 cup buttermilk
3 Tablespoons oil
1 Tablespoon vanilla extract
2 large eggs, at room temperature
2 large egg whites, at room temperature
1-¼ cups sugar

MAPLE MERINGUE FROSTING
1 Tablespoon water
1 teaspoon vanilla extract
1 teaspoon unflavored gelatin
2 large egg whites
½ cup High Acres maple syrup
¼ teaspoon cream of tarter
Pinch of salt
DRIZZLE & FINAL FANCYING
½ cup High Acres maple syrup
⅓ cup walnuts
• Preparation
TO MAKE CAKE:
Preheat over to 325ºF. Grease and flour two 9-inch round cake pans. Spread nuts in a shallow pan and bake for 4 to 6 minutes, or until fragrant. Let cool. In a food processor, combine toasted nuts, flour, baking powder, baking soda and salt; process until nuts are finely ground. Set aside. In a glass-measuring cup, combine buttermilk, oil and vanilla; set aside. In a large mixing bowl, combine eggs, egg whites and sugar. Beat with an electric mixer at high speed until mixture is thick and pale, about 5 minutes. With a rubber spatula, alternately fold dry ingredients and buttermilk mixture into egg mixture. Divide batter between prepared pans and bake for 25 to 35 minutes, or until tops spring back when touched lightly. Let cool in pans on a wire rack for 5 minutes. Loosen edges and invert into rack and let cool completely.
TO MAKE FROSTING:
In a small bowl, combine water and vanilla. Sprinkle with gelatin and let soften for 1 minute. In a wide pot, bring about 1 inch of water to a bare simmer. In a heatproof mixing bowl large enough to fit over the pot, combine egg whites, ½ cup maple syrup, cream of tartar and salt. Set bowl over barely simmering water and beat with an electric mixer on low speed, moving beaters constantly, until an instant-read thermometer registers 140ºF. (This will take 3 to 5 minutes.) Increase mixer speed to high and continue beating for 3½ minutes. Remove bowl from heat. Add gelatin mixture and continue to beat until cooled to room temperature, 4 to 5 minutes more.
TO ASSEMBLE & DECORATE CAKE:

Fill and frost the two-layer cake, covering top and sides. Cover loosely and refrigerate for at least 1 hour or up to 8 hours. No more than 1 hour before serving, place a large shallow bowl of water beside stove. Pour remaining ½ cup maple syrup into a small saucepan and being to a boil. Reduce heat to low and boil gently, without stirring, until a drop of syrup immersed in cold water forms a thread between your fingers, 5 to 10 minutes. Immediately dip base of saucepan in water to arrest cooking and cool syrup quickly. When syrup has cooled and thickened slightly, use a spoon to drizzle over cake (rewarm over low heat if syrup has hardened). Chop remaining ⅓ cup nuts. Using a flat metal spatula or pastry scraper, press nuts around bottom half of cake.

**Upside Down Maple Apple Gingerbread Cake**
• Ingredients
1 cup High Acres maple syrup
2 Tablespoons butter, melted
½ cup seedless raisins
2 medium apples, cored, pared and sliced
½ cup sugar
1 fresh egg
1-½ cups sifted flour
1 teaspoon baking soda
¾ teaspoon ginger
1 teaspoon salt
½ cup butter, melted
½ cup boiling water
• Preparation
Preheat oven to 350°F. Combine butter and ½ cup syrup and pour into greased 9" square cake pan. Scatter raisins over the mixture and arrange the sliced apples. Combine ½ cup syrup and sugar and beat in the egg. Combine flour, baking soda, spices and salt and beat into syrup mixture. Combine melted shortening and boiling water, add to batter and beat well. Pour batter over apple slices and bake for 45 minutes. Turn out onto serving platter and serve warm topped with whipped cream or ice cream.

CHEESECAKES

**Maple Praline Cheesecake**
• Ingredients
¼ cup butter
1 cup graham cracker crumbs
2 Tablespoons brown sugar
24 ounces cream cheese
1-¼ cups brown sugar
2 Tablespoons flour
4 eggs
1-½ teaspoons vanilla
½ cup pecans, chopped
3 Tablespoons High Acres maple syrup
• Preparation
Crust: Melt butter in saucepan. Stir in graham cracker crumbs and sugar. Pack into bottom of ungreased 9" spring-form pan. Bake at 350°F for 10 minutes. Filling: Beat cheese, sugar and flour together at medium speed until blended. Add eggs, one at a time, beating until blended after each addition. Mix in vanilla and nuts. Pour over crust. Bake at 350°F for 50 to 60 minutes until firm. Chill.

**Maple Pumpkin Cheesecake**
• Ingredients
1-¼ cups graham cracker crumbs
¼ cup sugar
¼ cup butter, melted
3 (8 oz.) packages softened cream cheese
1 (14 oz.) can sweetened condensed milk (NOT evaporated milk)
1 (15 oz.) can pumpkin (about 1-¾ cups)
3 eggs
¼ cup High Acres maple syrup
1-½ teaspoons ground cinnamon
1 teaspoon ground nutmeg
½ teaspoon salt
Whipped cream and pecan halves, optional.
• Preparation

Preheat oven to 325°F. Combine crumbs, sugar and butter: press firmly on bottom of 9" spring-form pan. With mixer, beat cream cheese until fluffy. Gradually beat in condensed milk until smooth. Add pumpkin, eggs, syrup, cinnamon, nutmeg and salt; mix well. Pour into prepared pan. Bake 1-¼ hours or until center appears nearly set when shaken. Cool one hour. Cover and chill at least four hours. To serve, garnish with whipped cream and pecan. Store leftovers covered in refrigerator.

**Maple Walnut Cheesecake**
• Ingredients
CRUST:
1-½ cups graham cracker or vanilla wafer crumbs
5 Tablespoons butter, melted
2 Tablespoons sugar
FILLING:
1 (8-ounce) package cream cheese, softened
1 (14-ounce) can sweetened condensed milk
⅓ cup lemon juice
2 Tablespoons High Acres maple syrup
TOPPING:
1 cup High Acres maple syrup
½ cup water
1 egg, beaten
1-½ Tablespoons cornstarch
½ cup chopped walnuts
• Preparation
To make the crust combine the graham cracker or vanilla wafer crumbs, sugar and butter. Mix well. Press into a 9" pie pan. Chill the crust while you make the filling. To make the filling, beat the cream cheese until fluffy. Add the milk, lemon juice and 2 Tablespoons maple syrup; beat well. Pour into the prepared piecrust. Chill for several hours. To make the topping, bring the 1 cup maple syrup and ½ cup water to a boil. Mix together the egg and cornstarch. Add a little bit of the boiling syrup to the mixture so the egg doesn't cook before incorporating it all together. Stir and cook until the syrup is thickened. Spread over the cream cheese filling. Garnish with the chopped walnuts. Keep refrigerated until served.

FROSTINGS and FILLINGS

## Maple Cream Filling for Cakes, Cream Puffs or Twinkies
• Ingredients
1 cup heavy cream
⅜ cup High Acres maple syrup
Pinch salt
• Preparation
Beat all together until stiff.

## Maple Frosting
• Ingredients
¼ cup softened butter
2 cups sifted powdered sugar
High Acres maple syrup
• Preparation
Cream butter, and gradually add powdered sugar. Stir in enough maple syrup until mixture is of spreading consistency.

## Maple Nut Butter Frosting
• Ingredients
½ cup butter
¼ cup chopped walnuts or pecans
3 cups powdered sugar
4 to 6 Tablespoons High Acres maple syrup
• Preparation
Thoroughly cream butter and sugar, and add maple syrup until light and spreadable. Add nuts and frost cake.

FROZEN DESSERTS
(INCLUDING, OF COURSE, ICE CREAM)

## Frozen Maple Chocolate Marshmallow Delight
• Ingredients
2 cups vanilla wafer crumbs
¼ cup melted butter
1-½ cups powdered sugar
½ cup butter
3 eggs

3 squares unsweetened melted chocolate
1-½ cups whipped cream
½ cup High Acres maple syrup
1 package (10 oz) small marshmallows
1 cup chopped pecans
• Preparation
Line an 8" square pan with waxed paper, allowing edges to extend above pan. Blend together crumbs and butter. Press crumb mixture in bottom of pan. Cream powdered sugar and ½ cup butter thoroughly. Add eggs, one at a time, and melted chocolate. Beat until light and fluffy. Spoon mixture over crumbs and set in freezer. Combine whipping cream and maple syrup. Chill in refrigerator for ½ hour. Whip until stiff. Gently fold in marshmallows and ⅔ cup nuts. Spread over chocolate mixture. Sprinkle with remaining nuts. Freeze firmly. Remove from pan. (Can be lifted out with the extending wax paper). Cut as many squares as needed and return unused portion, wrapped, to freezer.

**Frozen Maple Mousse**
• Ingredients
2 eggs, separated
¼ cup sugar
¾ cup whipping cream
½ cup High Acres maple syrup, divided as follows:
• Preparation
Bowl 1: Beat egg yolks with sugar and ¼ cup maple syrup until light and fluffy. Heat remaining ¼ cup maple syrup until boiling. Set aside to cool until just warm. Bowl 2: Beat egg whites until stiff; gradually add warm syrup. Bowl 3: Whip cream into stiff peaks. Mix all 3 bowls and fill individual serving dishes. Freeze for at least 4 hours.

**Frozen Maple Walnut Mousse Pie**
• Ingredients
3 eggs, separated
⅛ teaspoon salt
¾ cup High Acres maple syrup
2 cups Cool Whip
1 cup walnuts, chopped

2 Tablespoons semi-sweet chocolate, shaved
1 chocolate crumb pie shell
• Preparation
Beat egg yolks until lemon colored. Add salt and maple syrup. Cook in top of double boiler until yolk mixture thickens. Cool. Beat egg whites until stiff. Combine maple mixture, egg whites, and ⅔ of the cool whip, using a folding motion. Fold in ¾ cup of the nutmeats. Scrape into baked pie shell. Cover with remaining whipped topping. Sprinkle with remaining nutmeats and chocolate shavings. Freeze for a minimum or four hours.

## Maple Ginger Ice Cream
• Ingredients
1 cup light cream
3 Tablespoons High Acres maple syrup
4 Tablespoons confectioner sugar
2 teaspoons vanilla extract
¾ cup heavy cream
½ cup milk
2 teaspoons white rum (optional)
1 cup stem ginger, drained and finely chopped
• Preparation
Whisk the heavy cream and maple syrup until stiff. Gently heat the light cream, vanilla extract, confectioner sugar and milk in a heavy saucepan, stirring continuously until sugar is dissolved, then stir in the heavy cream mixture. Pour into container and freeze for approximately 2 hours until mushy. Turn into a chilled bowl, beat with whisk, and add the finely chopped ginger and rum (optional). Return to the container and freeze until firm. Serve with High Acres maple syrup.

## Maple Ice Cream Pie
• Ingredients
9" baked pie shell
1 quart vanilla ice cream, softened
¾ cup dark amber High Acres maple syrup
Whipped cream for garnish
Walnut halves for garnish
• Preparation

Combine vanilla ice cream and maple syrup in bowl until smooth. Pour into the crust and place in the freezer for 3 to 4 hours until frozen solid. Remove from freezer 20–15 minutes before serving. Garnish with whipped cream and walnuts.

## Maple Walnut Ice Cream
• Ingredients
1 quart cream
Pinch of salt
½ cup granulated High Acres maple sugar
½ cup chopped walnuts
½ cup brown sugar
¼ cup High Acres maple syrup
• Preparation
Scald the cream, dissolving into ½ cup brown sugar and ¼ cup maple syrup and the salt. Chill overnight in a glass container. Freeze in a crank ice cream freezer, adding nuts and chopped hard maple sugar before the last 20 cranks. Pack and freeze until hard.

## Captain Art's Shipwreck Sundae
• Ingredients
Thick, dark maple syrup, cooled
Vanilla ice cream (He uses Ben & Jerry's exclusively!)
Frozen waffles (the life raft)
• Preparation
Build the sundae on a plate. Toast waffles. While waffle is hot, place ice cream and syrup on top.

PIES and CRISPS

## Apple Crisp
• Ingredients
FILLING
6 cups apples, chopped
1 teaspoon cinnamon
1-½ Tablespoons whole wheat flour
TOPPING
6 Tablespoons High Acres maple syrup
1 cup whole wheat flour

½ cup oatmeal
¼ teaspoon salt
¼ teaspoon baking soda
⅓ cup oil
• Preparation
Toss apples with ¼ teaspoon cinnamon and 1-½ Tablespoons flour in baking dish. Drizzle with 3 Tablespoons maple syrup. In a separate bowl combine the flour, oats, salt, baking soda, and rest of cinnamon. Mix in oil and drizzle on the remaining maple syrup. Mix with fork and spread over apples. Bake at 350ºF for 45 minutes (or until apples are tender).

**Apple Custard Pie**
• Ingredients
4 cups thinly sliced apples
1 lemon, juice only
1 unbaked 9" pie crust
4 eggs
⅓ cup High Acres maple syrup
1 cup yogurt
1 teaspoon vanilla
1 teaspoon cinnamon
½ teaspoon nutmeg
¼ teaspoon salt
• Preparation
Slice apples, place in bowl with lemon juice. Combine all remaining ingredients in a blender and blend until frothy. Place apples in pie crust. Pour liquid over apples and bake at 375ºF for 45 minutes, or until solid in center. Cool thoroughly before serving (one hour or more).

**Bean and Maple Syrup Pie**
• Ingredients
1 cup well cooked white pea beans
½ cup High Acres maple syrup
2 eggs
⅓ cup brown sugar
⅓ cup melted butter
½ cup raisins or chopped pecans
One 9" unbaked pastry pie shell or 18 unbaked tart shells

Pecan halves (optional)
● Preparation
Puree beans in food processor or blender with maple syrup until smooth. Add eggs, sugar and butter and mix just until well blended. Sprinkle raisins or chopped pecans in bottom of pie or tart shells. Pour filling on top of raisins or chopped pecans. Garnish with pecan halves if desired. Bake pie in a 350ºF oven for 35 to 40 minutes or tarts for 20 minutes or until set in center. Cool. Serve at room temperature plain or with whipped cream or ice cream.

## Maple Apple Crunch
● Ingredients
BASE
4-½ cups peeled and sliced apples
2 Tablespoons all-purpose flour
¾ cup white sugar
½ cup High Acres maple syrup
1 teaspoon cinnamon
TOPPING
1-½ cups oatmeal
1-½ cups all-purpose flour
½ cup High Acres maple syrup
¾ cup melted butter
1 teaspoon baking soda
1 teaspoon baking powder
½ cup chopped walnuts
● Preparation
For base, mix all ingredients and put in an ungreased 9"x 12" baking dish. Combine topping ingredients and spread on top of base. Bake 40 minutes at 350ºF. Serve with ice cream or whipped cream and High Acres maple syrup.

## Maple Caramel Candy Pie
● Ingredients
2 cups graham cracker crumbs
⅓ cup High Acres maple syrup
⅓ cup butter, melted
¼ cup butter, second amount
1 cup caramels, preferably maple flavored (30-32)

1 cup milk, warmed
3 large egg yolks
1 envelope unflavored gelatin
3 Tablespoons cold water
¼ cup boiling water
½ cup heavy cream
3 Tablespoons High Acres maple syrup
● Preparation

Preheat oven to 375ºF. Prepare crust by mixing together graham crackers crumbs, ⅓ maple syrup and melted butter. Pat into a lightly greased 9"pie plate and bake 8 minutes. Remove from oven and set aside to cool. Over boiling water in a double boiler combine second amount of butter, caramels and warm milk. Cook, stirring constantly, until caramels are melted and mixture comes to a boil. Remove from stove and immediately whisk in egg yolks, stirring until fully incorporated. Sprinkle gelatin over cold water and allow to soften, approximately 5 minutes. Stir boiling water into gelatin, and then fold into caramel mixture. Pour into prepared crust, cover with plastic wrap and refrigerate until firm, approximately 3-4 hours. At serving time, whip heavy cream until soft peaks form. Gently whip in 3 Tablespoons maple syrup and continue to beat until cream stiffens. Cut pie in wedges and serve with a dollop of maple flavored whipped cream.

**Maple Pecan Pie**
● Ingredients
¼ cup butter
½ teaspoon salt
3 eggs
1 unbaked 9" pastry shell
½ cup sugar
1 cup High Acres maple syrup
1 cup broken pecan halves
● Preparation

Melt butter; add sugar, salt, maple syrup and eggs. Beat the mixture until well blended. Add the pecans, breaking large halves in two. Pour filling into the unbaked shell. Bake at 375ºF for about 35 minutes or until a knife inserted in the filling comes out clean. Cool pie before serving.

**Maple Pie**
• Ingredients
1 each 8" piecrust
1-½ cups packed light brown sugar
2 large eggs at room temperature
½ cup heavy cream
⅓ cup High Acres maple syrup (preferably dark amber)
2 teaspoons unsalted butter, melted
• Preparation
Preheat oven to 350°F. Whisk together brown sugar and eggs until creamy. Add cream, syrup, and butter, then whisk until smooth. Pour filling into pie shell. Bake pie in lower third of oven until pastry is golden and filling is puffed and looks dry but still trembles, 50 to 60 minutes. Cool on a rack to room temperature (filling will set as pie cools). Garnish with whipped cream.

**Maple Rhubarb Pie**
• Ingredients
3 cups rhubarb, cut up
1 egg
2 Tablespoons flour (rounded)
⅔ cup High Acres maple syrup
⅔ cup sugar
Pinch of salt
2-crust pie shell
• Preparation
Beat egg; add sugar, syrup, and flour. Mix well and add rhubarb. Put into two-crust pie. Bake at 425°F for 15 minutes. Reduce heat to 350°F until it bubbles, approximately 30 minutes.

**Coconut Custard Pie**
• Ingredients
3 eggs
¼ cup sugar
1 cup High Acres maple syrup
2-½ Tablespoons flour
Scant ⅛ teaspoon Salt

77

1 teaspoon vanilla
1-¼ cups whole milk
¼ cup melted butter or margarine
¼ cup quick oatmeal
½ cup sweetened flakes coconut
½ cup chopped walnuts
Pastry for a 9" 1-crust pie
• Preparation
Preheat oven to 350ºF. Beat eggs and sugar together. Add other ingredients, beating in oatmeal, coconut, and the nuts last. Pour into pie shell and bake at 350ºF for 40 minutes.

## Sue Melanson's Maple Syrup Apple Pie
• Ingredients
1 two-crust pie pastry, your favorite, but add the grated rind of one small lemon
5 tart apples, peeled, cored and sliced
½ cup of High Acres maple syrup
½ teaspoon nutmeg
½ teaspoon cinnamon
1 Tablespoon butter
Optional: walnuts and/or raisins
• Preparation
Place the bottom crust in a greased pie dish and fill with the apples. Heat together, the maple syrup, spices and butter just until butter is melted. Whisk to blend. Pour over the apples. Put top crust in place, seal edges and cut vents. (I use a mini-apple cookie cutter in the shape of a small maple leaf to create the vents on the top crust before placing on top of the pie. I lay the cutout pieces next to the vents to add visual interest and pie identification). Bake 45 minutes to an hour at 350ºF.

PUDDINGS and MOUSSES
(IN MAINE WE CALL THEM "MOOSES")

## Apple Batter Pudding
• Ingredients
4 large tart apples
½ cup High Acres maple syrup
¼ cup boiling water

5 Tablespoons butter or margarine
½ teaspoon baking powder
¼ cup flour
1 egg, beaten
• Preparation
Peel, core and slice apples into a deep pudding dish. Pour maple syrup and boiling water over the slices and dot with 2 Tablespoons of the butter. Make a batter of remaining ingredients: Beat egg, and add sugar beating well. Add 1 Tablespoon butter and baking powder and flour. Mix well and spread over apple mixture and dot with last 2 Tablespoons. Bake at 400°F until apples are soft, 45-50 minutes.

**Blueberry Maple Bread Pudding
with Lemon Whipped Cream**
• Ingredients
¾ cup heavy cream
¼ teaspoon grated lemon peel
2 Tablespoons powdered sugar
1-½ Tablespoons fresh lemon juice or enough to taste
¾ cup half & half
¼ cup of High Acres maple syrup
½ teaspoon vanilla
2 large eggs
4 cups French bread cubes
1 cup blueberries, fresh or frozen
• Preparation
Lemon Whipped Cream: In a medium bowl, beat ½ cup heavy cream at medium speed. As cream begins to thicken, add grated lemon peel and powdered sugar. Drizzle in the lemon juice and whip until stiff. Refrigerate. Bread Pudding: In a medium bowl, whisk together remaining ¼ cup cream, half- &-half, maple syrup, vanilla and eggs. In a large bowl, pour cream mixture over bread cubes; mix well. Fold in blueberries. Pour into a 2-quart baking dish. Refrigerate 15 to 30 minutes. Preheat oven to 350°F. Bake uncovered until set, about 30-40 minutes. Serve warm with lemon whipped cream on top.

**Chocolate Tofu Grand Marnier Pudding**
• Ingredients
10 oz silken soft tofu
¼ cup cocoa powder
2 to 4 Tablespoons High Acres maple syrup
2 to 3 Tablespoons Grand Marnier liqueur
1 teaspoon vanilla extract
• Preparation
Drain the tofu in a fine-mesh strainer for 15 minutes. In a blender or food processor, puree the tofu until creamy, about 30 seconds. Add the cocoa powder, maple syrup, Grand Marnier, and the vanilla extract. Blend thoroughly, scraping down the sides of the container. Blend until the mixture is extremely smooth. Transfer to a well-sealed container and refrigerate at least 1 hour. Will keep for up to three days.

**Decadently Rich Maple Bread Pudding**
• Ingredients
½ pound rich bread, crust removed and cut in ½ inch cubes
(I use Portugese Sweet Bread or Challaugh Bread.)
12 large egg yolks
1 cup plus 2 Tablespoons High Acres maple syrup
4 cups heavy cream
• Preparation
Cut bread in cubes and toast until golden brown. Spread evenly in pan. Whisk together yolks and syrup. Heat cream until hot to touch. Gradually whisk cream into egg mixture and strain over bread. Place plastic over bread to submerge. Let stand until bread is soaked. Cover with foil and bake in water bath for one hour and 15 minutes or until custard is set (350ºF oven). Drizzle with warm syrup and serve.

**Maple Bread Pudding**
• Ingredients
¾ cup High Acres maple syrup
1 teaspoon lemon juice
3 slices bread without crusts
2 eggs
2 cups milk

1 Tablespoon butter
¼ teaspoon salt
½ cup nutmeats or raisins
¼ teaspoon vanilla
• Preparation
Pour maple syrup into the top of a double boiler. Butter each slice of bread and cube them. Add to syrup then add nuts or raisins and juice. Beat together eggs, milk, salt and vanilla. Then pour over the bread mixture. Do not stir. Set over gently boiling water. Cook 1 hour. This will make it's own sauce. Spoon the sauce over each serving.

## Maple Charlotte
• Ingredients
1 Tablespoon unflavored gelatin
¼ cup water
2 cups milk
3 eggs separated
⅛ teaspoon salt
1 cup High Acres maple syrup
• Preparation
Dissolve gelatin in water. Put the milk in a double boiler and sprinkle the dissolved gelatin on top. Heat to scalding, stirring until gelatin dissolves entirely. Beat egg yokes with salt, stirring in half the milk slowly. Return all to the double boiler and cook over hot water (not boiling) until mixture coats spoon. Remove from heat, stir in maple syrup and cool until mixture thickens. Then whip until light and frothy. Beat the egg whites stiff, and fold into the syrup and egg mixture, chill until firm.

## Maple Custard
• Ingredients
4 eggs, separated
¾ cup High Acres maple syrup
4 cups milk
¾ cup chopped nutmeats
⅛ teaspoon salt
• Preparation
Beat yolks and syrup together. Add milk and nutmeats. Whip egg whites with salt until stiff. Fold the custard into the egg

whites. Fill up individual custard cups, place them in a pan of hot water and bake until custard is firm. Oven temp. 325° F.

## Maple Crème Brulee
- Ingredients
1 quart heavy cream
1 vanilla bean
½ cup sugar
9 egg yolks
⅓ cup High Acres maple syrup
Brown sugar for topping
- Preparation
Heat cream with vanilla bean and sugar on medium heat, while stirring, until sugar dissolves. Do not boil. Remove from heat and remove vanilla bean. Whisk egg yolks and maple syrup together. Slowly add cream to the egg mixture. Pour equal amounts of custard mixture into 8 individual ramekins. Place ramekins side by side in a roasting pan and fill with warm water half way up the sides of ramekins. Bake in preheated 350ºF oven for 45 minutes, until custard is set. Cool in refrigerator until serving time. Before serving, sprinkle top of each custard dish evenly with brown sugar and run under broiler until sugar caramelizes. (You can also use a blowtorch to caramelize the sugar topping.) Remove and serve.

## Maple Rice Pudding
- Ingredients
1 cup rice
2 cups milk
1 cup heavy cream
¾ cup High Acres maple syrup
Whipped cream
- Preparation
Cook rice in milk in top of double boiler until soft. Whip the cream and add the syrup to it gradually. Blend with the cooked rice. Place in a bowl or individual dishes and set in refrigerator to cool. Serve with whipped cream.

## Maple Walnut Parfait
- Ingredients

Vanilla ice cream (may substitute frozen vanilla yogurt)
Warm High Acres maple syrup
Walnuts, plain or maple toasted (recipe to follow)
Whipped sweet cream
• Preparation
Simply layer ingredients in clear tall parfait dishes. Topped with maple toasted walnuts.

**Maple Toasted Walnuts**
Chop walnuts coarsely, then, soak in pure maple syrup and layer on baking sheet. Bake for 20 minutes at 325°F. Allow to cool before serving.

**Microwave Maple Pudding**
• Ingredients
2 cups High Acres maple syrup
1 cup milk
1 egg
3 heaping teaspoons cornstarch
• Preparation
Mix syrup and egg well together. Dissolve the cornstarch in the milk. Mix together and put into a microwave bowl. Cook for 10 minutes at Level 8 (medium high level), stirring every 3 minutes.

**Oak Hill Farm Maple Mousse**
• Ingredients
1 envelope plus 2 teaspoons unflavored gelatin
½ cup cold water
4 egg yolks, well beaten
1 cup High Acres maple syrup
½ cup light brown sugar
4 egg whites
2 cups whipping cream, chilled
• Preparation
Sprinkle gelatin on water; let soften 5 minutes, then set cup in pan of hot water. Stir until gelatin dissolves. Add gelatin to beaten egg yolks, mix into maple syrup and cook over medium-low heat, stirring constantly, until mixture thickens and coats spoon.  Do not let mixture boil. Remove from heat and stir in

brown sugar, blending well. Transfer to a large bowl and cool to room temperature. Beat egg whites until they form stiff peaks. Whip cream only until stiff enough to hold its shape. With rubber spatula, fold cream gently into maple syrup mixture. Then fold in egg whites until whites no longer show. Spoon the mousse mixture into a 1-½ quart mold that has been rinsed in cold water. Cover top with plastic and chill at least 4 hours or until firm.

## Simple Maple Mousse
• Ingredients
3 egg yolks
¾ cup High Acres maple syrup
2 cups heavy cream
• Preparation
Beat egg yolks in the top of a double boiler (off heat) until lemon colored. Heat maple syrup to boiling point, pour very slowly into egg yolks, whisking continuously. Cook over boiling water until eggs coat a spoon (170ºF). Be careful not to heat mixture too fast. Cool mixture over ice while stirring constantly to room temperature. Beat chilled heavy cream stiff and doubled in volume. Fold in maple-egg mixture until well blended. Fill parfait glasses, Refrigerate until ready to use or freeze if it will be several days until you need them.

MISCELLANEOUS DESSERTS

## Cream Puffs with Maple Filling
• Ingredients
PUFFS
1 cup boiling water
½ cup butter
¼ teaspoon salt
1 cup sifted all purpose flour
4 eggs, unbeaten
• Ingredients
CREAM FILLING (page 70)
FROSTING (page 70)
• Preparation
PUFFS

84

Combine water, butter and salt in saucepan. Bring to a rolling boil, add flour all at once and stir over the heat until mixture leaves the sides of the pan and forms a ball. Remove from heat, and gradually beat in one egg at a time. Mix until it has a smooth texture. Drop by tablespoon onto a baking sheet. Bake at 425°F for 30 minutes, or until no beads of moisture can be seen on the puffs. When cool, cut off tops with a serrated knife, and fill with cream filling (page 70). Replace top and dust with powdered sugar, frost with maple frosting (page 70).

**Maine Maple Dumplings**
• Ingredients
DUMPLINGS
2 cups all-purpose flour
1 cup milk
4 teaspoons baking powder
4 Tablespoons butter
Pinch of salt
SYRUP
2 cups High Acres maple syrup
1 cup water
Pinch of salt
½ cup seedless raisins
• Preparation
Mix all-purpose flour, baking powder and salt. Sift together. Cut in butter with 2 knives or pastry blender. Add milk and stir to obtain a smooth paste. Drop thick dough, by spoonfuls, into boiling maple syrup and allow to cook 20 minutes without removing lid from the pan. Serve with maple syrup, thickened if desire, to which raisins have been added. It is very important to add milk to dry ingredients at the last minute when maple syrup is ready to start cooking dumplings.

## CHAPTER 9
## FRUIT

**Baked Apples**
Remove the cores to within ½" of the bottoms of 8 apples. Fill the apples with High Acres maple syrup and a dab or butter. Place them in a 13"x 9"x 2" pan with 1-½ cups of water. Bake at 375°F until the apples are tender, about 40-60 minutes. Baste occasionally with the maple syrup.

Microwave Variation:
2-2½ minutes for 1 apple
3-3½ minutes for 2 apples
4-4½ minutes for 3 apples
5-5½ minutes for 4 apples

**Grapefruit Grilled with Maple Syrup**
• Ingredients
2 grapefruit, cut in half
½ cup High Acres maple syrup
4 Tablespoons melted butter
Dash cinnamon
Handful golden raisins
• Preparation
Combine syrup, butter, and cinnamon, and spread over the cut half of each grapefruit (You may want to cut each section free before broiling). Sprinkle raisins on top. Place on broiler pan about 4" below flame and broil 2-4 minutes. Serve Hot.

**Hot Maple Syrup Peaches**
• Ingredients
2 to 3 sliced peaches
1 Tablespoon butter
½ cup High Acres maple syrup
2 teaspoons lemon juice
¼ teaspoon cinnamon
• Preparation
Preheat oven to 375° F. Place sliced peaches in oiled baking dish. Combine other ingredients and pour over the peaches. Cover and bake for 15 minutes. Uncover and bake 15 minutes

longer, basting the peaches occasionally. Serve warm over your favorite plain cake.

## Mashed Maple Syrup Apples
● Ingredients
4 Red Delicious apples
½ cup High Acres maple syrup
¾ cup coarsely chopped walnuts
¼ cup melted butter
1 teaspoon ground cinnamon
1 Tablespoon sugar
● Preparation
Preheat the oven to 400ºF. Use a small, unbuttered baking dish for baking the apples and a 9"x 4" loaf pan for the mashed mixture. Peel the apples and core them, using an apple corer, but leave them whole. Place them close together in the baking dish. Add ½ inch of water and bake until very soft, about 1 hour. Remove from the oven and let cool. Place in a medium bowl. Turn on the broiler to high. While the broiler is heating, add the maple syrup, walnuts, butter, and cinnamon to the apples. Mash everything together with a large fork. Scrape the mixture into the baking dish. Sprinkle the sugar on top. Broil until the top has caramelized to a rich brown, about 3 minutes. Note: Be sure to use Red Delicious apples. Different apples react differently. Serve over vanilla ice cream.

## Oranges with Maple Carmel
● Ingredients
2 medium Navel Oranges
¼ cup firmly packed light brown sugar
2 Tablespoons High Acres maple syrup
1 Tablespoon lemon juice
1 Tablespoon water
● Preparation
Peel oranges, and slice, or section. Divide between two dessert dishes. Bring to boiling sugar, maple syrup, lemon juice and water in small saucepan; cook 3 to 4 minutes until thick syrup forms. Spoon over oranges.

**Pears Spiced with Maple Syrup**
• Ingredients
6 ripe pears, peeled with stalks in place
6 cloves
8 cracked cardamom seeds
2 cinnamon sticks
1 Tablespoon sugar
6 Tablespoons High Acres maple syrup
1 cup medium/sweet white wine
• Preparation
Preheat oven to 400ºF. Push a clove inside each pear and lay on their sides with cinnamon sticks in an ovenproof dish. Scatter cardamom seeds on top of pears. Gently heat white wine, maple syrup and sugar until dissolved and pour over pears, ensuring they are half covered. Cover pears with foil and poach for approximately 1 hour or until tender, basting occasionally. Remove cloves, cardamom seeds and cinnamon before serving. Serves 6

**Summer Fruit Compote**
• Ingredients
½ cup High Acres maple syrup
2 cups water
1-½ cups halved & pitted plums
1 basket boysenberries
1 basket raspberries
2 peeled & sectioned naval oranges
Fresh mint leaves
1 peeled & sectioned grapefruit
½ lb. green seedless grapes
⅓ cup wine (plum is good)
• Preparation
In a saucepan, bring maple syrup and water to boil; simmer for two minutes. Reduce heat to low simmer and poach plums (submerge them in hot water) for 30 seconds. Transfer plums with slotted spoon to the serving bowl. Poach boysenberries and raspberries for 15 seconds, and then transfer them to serving bowl. Poach orange and grapefruit sections 1 minute, and remove them to the serving dish. Poach grapes for 15 seconds, and transfer them to the serving dish. Stir wine into

the syrup and simmer two minutes. Let wine syrup cool; spoon over fruit. Sprinkle compote with fresh mint leaves. Ladle into individual bowls. May be served alone, or with ice cream or yogurt.

## Wild Blueberry Crisp with Maple
• Ingredients
3 cups fresh or frozen wild blueberries
½ cup High Acres maple syrup
1 teaspoon cinnamon
⅓ cup cornstarch topping
1-½ cups flour
1 cup brown sugar
½ cup butter or margarine
1 teaspoon almond flavoring, optional
Powdered sugar
• Preparation
Combine wild blueberries, syrup, cinnamon and cornstarch, and spoon into an 8" well-greased baking pan. Mix flour and sugar. Cut in butter until mixture resembles coarse breadcrumbs. Stir in almond flavoring. Spread the topping evenly over berries, and Bake 25 to 30 minutes at 400ºF. Cool; sprinkle with powdered sugar. Serve with ice cream or whipped cream.

*The evaporator will boil down 40 gallons of sap to make one gallon of maple syrup.*

# CHAPTER 10
## JAMS, JELLIES, RELISH AND SPREADS

**Maple Butter**
• Ingredients
½ cup (1 stick) unsalted butter, softened
Pinch of salt
¼ cup High Acres maple syrup
• Preparation
With an electric mixer, whip the butter and salt until light and fluffy. With the mixer running, dribble the syrup into the butter while beating constantly. Adding the syrup slowly and beating constantly will prevent the mixture from separating. The spread may be refrigerated, in a covered container, for up to 3 weeks.

**Maple Cream**
• Ingredients
2 cups High Acres light amber maple syrup
• Preparation
In a heavy-bottom 4-quart pot, heat maple syrup on medium-high heat to 235°F, stirring the surface occasionally to keep it from boiling over. Immediately remove the pot from the heat, leaving the thermometer clipped to the side, and place the pot in a sink filled with cold water to cool it rapidly. (Do not touch the syrup while it is cooling, or large crystals will form.) When the mixture has cooled to approximately 125°F, remove the pot from the water and immediately beat the mixture with an electric mixer, scraping down the sides of the bowl. The syrup will gradually thicken, become lighter in color and begin to lose its glossy look. Continually test the consistency of mixture as you beat it by putting a little bit on your tongue and rolling it against the roof of your mouth. When it is ready, you will just begin to feel small crystals forming. Beating the mixture too long or failing to get it out of the pot in time will cause it to harden.

**Maple Cream Cheese Spread**
• Ingredients
½ cup High Acres maple syrup, the dark kind is fine
6 ounces cream cheese

• Preparation
Let the cheese soften at room temperature. Put the syrup in a small pan and simmer, stirring occasionally, over medium-low heat, until it is thickened to the texture of heavy honey, about 235° on a candy thermometer. Let it cool, stirring once or twice, and then beat into the cream cheese. You must reduce the syrup before combining it with the cheese or the mixture will curdle and separate. Store refrigerated, tightly covered and it will keep a long time.

## Maple Jelly
• Ingredients
½ gallon High Acres medium amber maple syrup
3 cups cold water
2 teaspoons Genugel (pectin does not work with maple syrup)
Genugel is available from maple syrup equipment suppliers.
• Preparation
Whisk the Genugel into the cold water first, and then add to syrup. Make sure the pot is at least 3 times the size of the liquid, as it foams up during boil. Boil all ingredients to 217.5°F. (Some people go to 219°F, but that makes unnecessarily hard jelly and wastes more content). The objective is to make clear jelly in the jar. Any infusion of air through stirring or filling of the jars will put air bubbles into the jelly. It will still taste fine, but won't look as good. Keep a low flame under the jelly while bottling, as this gels really fast and heat keeps it liquid longer. Skim off the surface foam, but take care not to be too fussy about it. Have a cup large enough to fill each clean jar with ONE pour. If you have to go back and add more to fill the jar, you will have air bubbles and layering. Cap the filled jars and process them in a hot water bath for 10 minutes at 180°F. A half gallon of syrup will net you five to seven 8 once jars of maple jelly.

## Maple Orange Cranberry Relish
• Ingredients
1 pound cranberries
2 oranges
1 cup High Acres maple syrup
• Preparation

Pick over and wash cranberries. Wash oranges, cut into quarters and remove white stringy pulp and seeds. Chop the cranberries and oranges fine. Add maple syrup. Mix thoroughly and let stand in refrigerator several days before using. More syrup may be added if a sweeter relish is desired.

**Persimmon Jam**
• Ingredients
1 cup seeded and chopped ripe persimmons
½ cup apricot juice
1 Tablespoon fresh lemon juice
1 teaspoon dried mint leaves, finely crumbled
½ teaspoon grated nutmeg
¼ teaspoon ground coriander seeds
½ Tablespoon High Acres maple syrup
• Preparation
Stir all the ingredients together in a medium-size heavy saucepan and bring the pot to a simmer over low heat. Simmer, covered, for 5 minutes, stirring often. Persimmon Jam will keep, tightly covered, in the refrigerator for 10 days or frozen for 6 months.

HAM

## Ham Balls in Peaches for the Ladies Who Lunch
• Ingredients
1 egg, beaten
½ cup soft breadcrumbs or crushed cereal
1 lb. cooked ham, ground
⅛ teaspoon ground cloves
½ cup High Acres maple syrup
1 teaspoon prepared mustard
12 peach halves, drained if canned
Parsley to garnish
High Acres maple syrup to baste
• Preparation
Preheat oven to 350°F. Combine egg, crumbs, maple syrup, cloves, mustard and ham. Shape into 12 balls. Drain peach halves and place a ham ball in center of each. Bake for 25 min. in a greased shallow pan. Baste once or twice with additional maple syrup to prevent drying out. Five minutes before baking time is up, garnish with chopped parsley.

## Ham Steak with Maple
• Ingredients
1 thick ham steak
¼ cup orange juice
3 to 4 Tablespoons High Acres maple syrup
• Preparation
Mix the orange juice and maple syrup. In a fry pan, brown the ham steak, turn it over, and drizzle ½ of the liquid onto the steak. Brown the other side, turn it over again, and spoon the remaining liquid over the steak. Cover and cook on low until done.

## Ham with Pineapple
• Ingredients
1 boneless ham (About 4-½ pounds)

4 cups cold water
4 cups apple juice
2 carrots, sliced
4 onions, chopped
1 garlic clove, finely crushed
4 celery stalks, sliced
1 Tablespoon prepared mustard
½ cup High Acres maple syrup
Orange marmalade
Pineapple slices
Cherries
Cloves
Fresh parsley, chopped finely
• Preparation
In a large pan, mix the water, juice, carrots, onions, garlic, celery, mustard and syrup. Bring to boil. Cover and let simmer for 30 minutes. In another pan, put the ham and cover. Let it simmer for 1 hour. Then let the ham cool down in its juices. Remove the ham from the pan. Remove most of the grease and any hard remnants. Preheat the oven 325°F. Place the ham in a dripping pan. Cover the bottom of the pan with some ham juice. Baste the ham with the marmalade. Decorate with the pineapple slices and cherries in the middle. Place cloves in the pineapple slices. Cover the pan and cook in the oven for 30-45 minutes, basting it with its juices from time to time. Remove the pan from the oven. Garnish with parsley and serve hot.

PORK

**Crispy Maple Spareribs**
• Ingredients
3 lbs lean pork spareribs
6 oz High Acres maple syrup
1 Tablespoon chili sauce
1 Tablespoon Worcestershire sauce
1 Tablespoon red wine vinegar
1 small onion, chopped
¼ teaspoon dry mustard

Salt
Freshly ground pepper
● Preparation
Roast ribs on a rack in pre-heated oven 400°F for 30 minutes. Combine the remaining ingredients in a pan and bring to a boil for 5 minutes. Remove ribs from rack and reduce heat to 350°F. Place ribs in a baking pan and cover with the sauce. Bake uncovered for a further 45 minutes, basting frequently.

## Maple Apple Stuffing for Crown Roast of Pork
● Ingredients
 1 medium onion, diced
¼ cup butter
3 medium apples, pared, cored and thinly sliced
2 Tablespoons High Acres maple syrup
3 Tablespoons boiling water
¼ teaspoons thyme
½ teaspoons poultry seasoning
1 teaspoon salt
⅛ teaspoons pepper
8 slices stale bread, cut into cubes
● Preparation
Simmer onion in butter for 5 minutes. Add apple slices, syrup, water, spices, salt and pepper. Cover and simmer until apples are barely tender, about 10 minutes. Turn mixture into large bowl and add the bread cubes. Toss lightly with fork.
Yield: Enough dressing for 6-7 pound crown roast of pork.

## Maple Barbecued Pork Spareribs
To reduce cooking time on the grill and thus the risk of burning, first parboil the ribs in boiling water for 10 minutes. Then marinate the cooked ribs for at least 8 hours or overnight and grill them for only about 10 minutes per side. WATCH these ribs closely as they burn easily.
● Ingredients
1 rack spareribs (about 4 pounds)
1 teaspoon freshly ground black pepper
½ teaspoon salt
⅔ cup High Acres maple syrup
2 Tablespoons rice-wine vinegar

1 Tablespoon soy sauce

• Preparation

Rub ribs with pepper and salt. Place in a shallow non-aluminum pan. In a small bowl, mix together maple syrup, vinegar and soy sauce. Pour over ribs, cover and chill overnight, turning occasionally. Remove ribs from pan and grill over moderately hot coals, turning and basting ribs so they cook evenly on both sides, about 20 minutes per side, or until done. Do not let them burn. Serves 4

## Maple Mustard Pork Tenderloin

• Ingredients

Pork tenderloin

3 teaspoons fresh sage, minced

Salt and pepper to taste

1 Tablespoon butter

1 cup low sodium chicken broth

2 Tablespoons High Acres maple syrup

2 Tablespoons coarse grain Dijon mustard

Fresh sage for garnish

• Preparation

Slice pork tenderloin into ⅓-inch thick slices. Sprinkle with 1-½ teaspoons sage, salt, and a generous amount of pepper. Melt butter in heavy medium skillet over medium-high heat. Add pork and cook until golden brown on both sides and cooked through, about 1-½ minutes per side. Transfer pork to plate, leaving drippings in skillet. Add broth, maple syrup, mustard, and remaining 1-½ teaspoons sage to skillet. Boil until syrupy and thick about 3 minutes, scraping up browned bits. Reduce heat to low. Return pork and any accumulated juices to skillet and cook until just heated through, about 1 minute. Serve pork with sauce. Garnish with fresh sage. Yield: about 4 servings

## Maple Pork Chops

• Ingredients

6 pork chops (1-inch thick)

¼ cup chopped onion

1 Tablespoon vinegar

1 Tablespoon Worchester sauce

1-½ teaspoons salt

½ teaspoon chili powder
⅛ teaspoon pepper
¼ cup High Acres maple syrup
¼ cup water
• Preparation
Preheat oven to 400°F. Lightly brown pork chops. Arrange in flat baking dish. Mix together onion, vinegar, Worcestershire Sauce, salt, chili powder, pepper, maple syrup and water. Pour over pork chops. Cover. Bake 45 minutes, basting occasionally. Uncover. Bake 15 minutes more. Remove chops to platter. Thicken sauce with flour. Pour over chops.

**Pork Chops Marinated in Maple Mustard Sauce**
• Ingredients
4 Center Cut Pork Chops 1 inch thick
Marinade:
⅓ cup High Acres maple syrup
⅓ cup Dijon mustard
2 Tablespoons molasses
1 teaspoon ground cumin
Salt & pepper to taste
Basting Sauce:
1 Tablespoon vinegar
½ teaspoon chili pepper
⅛ teaspoon pepper
¼ cup High Acres maple syrup
¼ cup water
1 Tablespoon Worchester sauce
1-½ teaspoons salt
Flour to thicken gravy
• Preparation
Preheat oven to 400°F. Lightly brown pork chops in a small amount of olive oil. Place chops in a flat baking dish. Combine all other ingredients over low heat and pour over chops. Cover and bake 45 minutes basting occasionally. Uncover and bake 15 minutes longer. Place chops on warming platter while sauce is thickened very slightly with flour. Pour sauce over chops and serve.

## Pork Medallions and Apples

• Ingredients

1 lb. pork tenderloin, cut crosswise into ¾" thick slices
1 teaspoon dried sage, divided
1 teaspoon salt divided
½ teaspoon pepper, divided
1 teaspoon oil, preferably olive
1 small onion, diced
1 clove garlic, minced
1 large sweet potato, peeled and cut into matchsticks
2 Granny Smith apples, cored and cut into ½" wedges
¼ cup apple juice
2 Tablespoons High Acres maple syrup
1 Tablespoon cider vinegar
1 Tablespoon chopped fresh cilantro or parsley

• Preparation

Using meat mallet pound pork slices between 2 sheets of wax paper or plastic wrap to ¼" thickness. Combine ½ Tablespoon sage, ½ teaspoon salt and ¼ teaspoon pepper; sprinkle over both sides of pork slices. Heat nonstick skillet over medium-high heat. Add pork, in batches if necessary, and cook turning once until lightly browned on both sides and no longer pink in center, 3-4 minutes per side. Remove from skillet: keep warm. In the same skillet, heat oil over medium-high heat. Add onion, garlic and remaining sage, salt and pepper. Cook until onion softens slightly, about 2 minutes. Add sweet potato and apples. Cook, stirring occasionally, until apples brown slightly, about 3 minutes. Add juice, syrup and vinegar. Cover; cook, stirring occasionally, until sweet potatoes and apples are tender, about 10 to 12 minutes. Add reserved pork slices; heat through, about 3 minutes. Serve sprinkled with cilantro or parsley

## Pork Spareribs in Maple Syrup

• Ingredients

3 lbs pork spareribs, cut in 5 2-inch length pieces
2 cups water
2 cups High Acres maple syrup
3 cloves chopped garlic
¼ cup lemon juice or cider vinegar

¼ cup Soy sauce
• Preparation
Combine all ingredients. Simmer over low heat until fully cooked.

**Pork Tenderloin Maple Syrup Shish Kebabs**
• Ingredients
SHISH KEBABS
1 lb pork tenderloin cubes
4 onions
4 apples
2 Tablespoons butter
MARINADE
1 cup High Acres maple syrup
¼ cup oil
¼ cup lemon juice or cider vinegar
¼ cup Soy sauce
Dry mustard
Curry powder
Parsley
• Preparation
Prepare marinade and let pork cubes marinate for 6 to 8 hours. Put cut apples, onions, and pork on skewers, and brush with oil. Add salt and pepper to taste. In a hot skillet (frying pan), sear skewers. Place skewers in hot oven 325°F for 30 minutes. Brush the Shish Kebabs with oil at least 4 times during cooking process. Serve over cooked rice.

*The finished syrup is put through a filter press for maximum clarity.*

## CHAPTER 12
## POULTRY

CHICKEN

### Chicken Breasts with Maple Horseradish Glaze
- Ingredients

4 to 6 pieces of chicken breast
4 to 6 strips of bacon, 1 per chicken piece
¼ cup High Acres maple syrup
¼ teaspoon horseradish
- Preparation

Mix syrup and horseradish. Wrap each chicken piece with a strip of bacon and secure with a toothpick. Place on broiler pan, brush with syrup, and broil 3 minutes. Turn, brush, and broil 2-3 minutes more, until bacon is crisp. Serve hot.

### Chicken Breasts with Maple Mustard Sauce
- Ingredients

2 Tablespoons vegetable oil
2 boneless and skinless chicken breasts,
        tossed in seasoned flour
½ cup sliced mushrooms
1 chopped scallions
½ cup heavy cream
3 Tablespoons High Acres maple syrup
1 teaspoon Dijon mustard
- Preparation

In a skillet (frying pan), heat oil and sauté chicken to a golden brown, then remove from pan and drain on a paper towel. In the skillet, quickly sauté the mushrooms and scallions. Add cream, maple syrup and mustard. Stir and cook until cream is reduced by half, or until sauce has a creamy consistency. Serve over chicken breasts. Serves 2

### Chicken in Maple Cream
- Ingredients

2 to 3 lb. chicken, cut up into serving pieces
1 egg, beaten
¼ cup milk

¾ cup corn flake crumbs
5 Tablespoons cooking oil
1 cup light cream
1 cup milk
½ cup High Acres maple syrup
• Preparation
Preheat oven to 375°F. Combine egg and milk. Put chicken pieces into this mixture and roll in crumbs. Brown chicken in hot oil and place pieces in shallow baking pan. Combine cream, milk and maple syrup and pour over chicken. Bake until tender (approximately 1-½ hours), turning once after ½ hour.

## Chicken Thighs with Maple Barbeque Glaze
• Ingredients
3 Tablespoons High Acres maple syrup
3 Tablespoons bottled chili sauce
1 Tablespoon cider vinegar
2 teaspoons dijon mustard
4 boneless chicken thighs
1 Tablespoon vegetable oil
• Preparation
Prepare barbeque (medium-high heat). Stir maple syrup, chili sauce, vinegar and mustard in small saucepan until well blended. Brush chicken with oil, season with salt and pepper. Arrange chicken on barbeque. Grill until cooked through, turning occasionally and brushing generously with sauce, about 10 minutes. Serve Immediately.

## Chicken with Golden Curry Sauce
• Ingredients
8 boneless, skinless, chicken breasts
¼ cup butter, melted
⅓ cup High Acres maple syrup
¼ cup Dijon mustard
1 Tablespoon yellow mustard
1 clove garlic, minced
1 Tablespoon fresh lemon juice
2 Tablespoons curry powder
1 teaspoon salt
½ cup finely chopped onion

• Preparation
Place the chicken in a 9" x 13" pan. Sprinkle chopped onion over chicken. Mix rest of ingredients to make sauce. Pour over chicken. Cover and bake at 450°F for 20 minutes. Uncover and bake 20-30 minutes or until done. Serve over rice.

## Grilled Breast of Chicken with Maple Bourbon Glaze
• Ingredients
1 teaspoon dried chervil
1 teaspoon dried thyme
2 chicken breasts, boned, skinned, and split
½ cup High Acres maple syrup
3 Tablespoons bourbon
1 Tablespoon vegetable oil
• Preparation
 Mix the chervil and thyme together in a small bowl. Rub generously over the surface of each chicken breast half. Transfer to a shallow baking dish. Combine the maple syrup, bourbon, and vegetable oil and pour over the chicken. Turn the chicken to coat both sides. Cover the dish with foil and marinate in the refrigerator for 1 hour. Grill the chicken over hot coals. Baste frequently with the marinade to create a shiny brown glaze.

## Grilled Chicken with Maple Sauce
• Ingredients
1 chicken, 3 to 4 pounds
½ cup vegetable oil
¼ cup wine vinegar
1 Tablespoon Soy sauce
1 Tablespoon finely chopped fresh ginger
2 cloves garlic, minced
¼ cup High Acres maple syrup
2 Tablespoons lemon juice
(Maple Sauce, recipe follows)
• Preparation
Rinse and pat dry the chicken, cut into 4 to 6 serving pieces. Combine remaining ingredients and marinate chicken, cover and refrigerate, for up to 24 hours. Turn chicken pieces to ensure that they are covered with the marinade. Preheat oven

to 400°F. Place chicken in an ovenproof dish and bake until tender, approximately 40-50 minutes. Baste occasionally with pan juices. Serve Maple Sauce over chicken.

MAPLE SAUCE
• Ingredients
½ cup High Acres maple syrup
3 Tablespoons butter, at room temperature
1 Tablespoon soy sauce
1 clove garlic, finely chopped
Salt, pepper, and cayenne to taste
• Preparation
While chicken is baking combine maple syrup, butter, soy sauce and garlic in a small saucepan and bring to boil. Reduce heat and simmer until sauce is reduced to half and thickened. Season to taste with salt, pepper and cayenne. Yields ⅓ cup sauce.

## Maple Chicken with Lemon and Almonds
• Ingredients
1 chicken, 2-½ to 3 pound cut-up
¼ cup melted butter
¼ cup High Acres maple syrup
½ teaspoon grated lemon rind
1 teaspoon salt
Dash of pepper
¼ cup chopped almonds
2 teaspoons lemon juice
• Preparation
Place the chicken pieces in a shallow, buttered baking dish. Mix remaining ingredients and pour evenly over chicken. Bake uncovered, 50-60 minutes, at 325 °F. Baste occasionally. Serve with rice.

## Maple Sweet & Sour Chicken
• Ingredients
¼ cup High Acres maple syrup
2 Tablespoons cornstarch
½ teaspoon salt
¾ cup juice drained from canned pineapple
¼ cup vinegar

1 Tablespoon soy sauce
3 cups cooked, sliced chicken
¼ cup thinly sliced onion
1 cup drained canned pineapple chunks
½ cup thinly sliced celery strips, 1-inch long
2 Tablespoons diced pimento
2 cups cooked rice
1 can or package of Chow Mein noodles
¼ cup slivered toasted almonds (optional)
• Preparation
Combine maple syrup, cornstarch and salt. Stir into pineapple liquid. Add vinegar and soy sauce. Bring liquids to boil over high heat and reduce heat, cooking until thick. Stir occasionally. Remove from heat and add chicken, onion, pineapple, and celery. Cook over medium heat for about 8 to 10 minutes, stirring occasionally. Add pimento and cook one minute longer. Serve over rice, sprinkle with almonds and top with noodles. Yield: 4 to 6 servings

## Rosemary Chicken with Orange Maple Glaze
• Ingredients
½ cup High Acres maple syrup
1 cup fresh orange juice
½ cup dry white wine (Do not use cooking wine)
2 teaspoons fresh garden rosemary, chopped
½ teaspoon salt
½ teaspoon black pepper, freshly ground
4 skinless, boneless chicken breast halves
2 Tablespoons fresh butter
2 Tablespoons olive oil
• Preparation
Bring orange juice and wine to a boil in a small saucepan. Reduce heat slightly, but continue a low boil for 5 minutes, stirring occasionally. Stir in maple syrup and continue boiling for another 5 to 6 minutes, stirring frequently, until glossy and just slightly thickened. Set this saucepan aside. In a small bowl mix together the fresh rosemary, salt and pepper. Rub mixture on both sides of chicken breasts, and set aside. Melt butter and olive oil in a large skillet over medium high heat. Add chicken breasts, cover skillet and sauté for about 5 minutes on each

side until lightly browned. Pour orange maple mixture over chicken (mixture will boil and bubble). Reduce heat to simmer; cover and let cook for another 10 minutes, basting occasionally, until chicken is cooked through and sauce has turned into a rich, thick glaze. Serve over rice and spoon rich glaze sauce over the top.

## Spicy Chicken Wings
• Ingredients
12 to 14 Chicken Wings
1 cup High Acres Maple Syrup
¼ teaspoon ground ginger
1 teaspoon minced garlic
1 Tablespoon cornstarch
¼ cup cider vinegar
2 Tablespoons soy sauce
• Preparation
Mix ingredients together and marinate chicken wings for 24 hours. Bake at 370°F for one hour in the marinade, basting often.

DUCK

## Maple-Spice Glazed Duck Breasts
• Ingredients
¼ cup sugar
1 Tablespoon salt
½ cup hot water
8 black peppercorns
4 whole bay leaves
2 whole cloves
½ teaspoon dried thyme
1 cup dark High Acres maple syrup
4 boneless duck breast halves, skin removed
(Pork tenderloin makes a good substitute.)
1 teaspoon ground allspice
2 teaspoons freshly ground black pepper
2 Tablespoons duck fat (or 1 Tablespoon butter plus 1 Tablespoon oil)
• Preparation

In a roomy bowl, make a brine by combining sugar, salt, and hot water; stir vigorously until dissolved. Add peppercorns, bay leaves, cloves, thyme, and maple syrup. Stir and then add duck breasts. Cover bowl and refrigerate at least 2 hours, turning the duck occasionally. Remove duck from brine and pat dry with paper towels. Dust with allspice and black pepper; set aside. Transfer brine to a small saucepan and simmer over medium to medium-low heat until it makes a thick, syrupy glaze. Meanwhile, heat duck fat (or butter-and-oil mixture) over high heat in a heavy bottomed sauté pan. When the fat in the pan is very hot, but not smoking, add the duck. Cook until brown on both sides, then reduce heat to medium. Begin basting the breasts with the glaze, turning frequently, until the glaze begins to dry out and caramelize. Cook 5 to 8 minutes longer, or until the duck breasts are firm and springy to the touch. Don't worry if the glaze blackens a little bit. Transfer the duck breasts to a cutting board and slice on a bias. Yield: 4 servings

TURKEY

**Maple Roasted Turkey with Riesling Wine Gravy**
• Ingredients
14 lb. fresh turkey, neck & giblets removed (reserve for stock)
Salt
Freshly ground black pepper
Corn Bread or Sourdough Stuffing (or your favorite)
6 Tablespoons unsalted butter
1 Tablespoon freshly grated ginger
¼ cup High Acres maple syrup
1-½ Tablespoons all-purpose flour
1 cup Riesling wine
2 cups homemade turkey stock (or canned)
⅔ cup seedless red and green grapes, each cut in half
• Preparation
Heat oven to 425ºF with rack in lowest third of oven. Wash turkey inside and out with cold running water, and pat dry with paper towels. Tuck wing tips under body. Generously season neck, body cavities and underside with salt and pepper. Loosely fill the neck cavity with the stuffing. Using wooden skewers or toothpicks, secure the flap. Holding the turkey

upright, loosely fill the body cavity with stuffing. Pull the legs together, and tie them with kitchen twine. Heap on additional stuffing so that it is bulging out of the cavity. Generously sprinkle salt and pepper over the bird, and set it on a rack in a roasting pan. Cut a double layer of cheesecloth to fit over the entire turkey. Melt 4 tablespoons butter. Place cheesecloth in the butter, completely soaking the cloth. Drape cheesecloth over the bird. Place turkey in the oven, and roast 30 minutes. Baste with butter that has accumulated in the pan. After the first 30 minutes of roasting, if no butter has accumulated in the roasting pan, melt four tablespoons unsalted butter and add three tablespoons turkey stock and baste with this mixture. Reduce heat to 350°F, and loosely cover bird with a large piece of aluminum foil; roast 30 minutes more. Baste again. Continue roasting, basting once an hour, until meat thermometer registers 180°F in the leg and 170° in the breast, about 3 hours for a 14-lb. bird. During the last half hour of roasting, place grated ginger in a small, double layer of cheesecloth; squeeze juice into a small saucepan. Add maple syrup and 1 tablespoon butter. Heat the mixture until the butter has melted and is bubbling. Remove the maple-syrup glaze from heat. Remove foil tent and cheesecloth from bird, and discard. Brush glaze over bird several times during last half hour. Remove turkey from the oven, and transfer to a carving board. Let rest 30 minutes before carving. In a small bowl, combine the remaining 1-tablespoon butter with flour, and mix together until smooth. Set aside. Pour pan drippings into a fat separator or glass-measuring cup, and let stand 10 minutes. If using a fat separator, carefully return juices to pan, and discard fat. If using measuring cup, use a spoon to skim fat from top, and return juices to pan. Place the roasting pan on top of the stove over medium-high heat. Pour wine into the pan, and using a wooden spoon stir up any brown bits on bottom. Cook liquid until reduced by half, about 6 minutes. Add turkey stock, and cook until reduced again by half, about 7 minutes. Pass the gravy through a cheesecloth-lined sieve, and pour into a small saucepan. Whisk in the reserved butter-flour mixture until the butter has melted. Reduce heat to medium-low, and let gravy simmer until slightly thickened, about 8 minutes. Add red and green grapes to the gravy; serve gravy with turkey.

**Coleslaw the Way We Do It In Maine**

• Ingredients

7 cups finely shredded cabbage (about a 1-pound head)

2 large tart apples, peeled, cored and shredded

1 small green pepper, chopped fine (optional)

Dressing:

2 Tablespoons vegetable oil

½ teaspoon powdered dry mustard

½ teaspoon salt

½ teaspoon black pepper

⅛ teaspoon cayenne pepper (optional)

1 Tablespoon plus 1 teaspoon cider vinegar

3 or 4 Tablespoons High Acres maple syrup

½ cup yogurt

• Preparation

In the bottom of a large bowl, combine the dressing ingredients in the order listed, using a wire whip to blend the mixture thoroughly. Toss in the vegetables, making sure they are evenly combined with each other and with the dressing. Cover tightly and refrigerate for at least a couple of hours so the flavor of the dressing has time to penetrate.

**Fruit Salad Dressing**

• Ingredients

¼ cup High Acres maple syrup

3 well-beaten egg yolks

Dash salt or pepper

Ginger

• Preparation

Bring maple syrup to boil. Combine with egg yolks. Cook 1 to 2 minutes over direct heat, stirring constantly from bottom of pan. Cool, and then season with salt or pepper. Add a few specs of ginger to taste.

**Ham and Lima Bean Salad with Maple Thyme Dressing**

• Ingredients

2 cups lima beans
3-½ teaspoons salt
1-½ pounds lean, smoky, baked ham, trim & cut into ½" cubes
1 cup vegetable oil
⅓ cup High Acres maple syrup
⅓ cup cider vinegar
3 Tablespoons finely minced fresh thyme
5 medium carrots, peeled and sliced thin
Freshly ground black pepper
1 head red-leaf lettuce, separated into leaves, washed, and patted dry
1 medium red onion, peeled and sliced into thin rings
• Preparation
In a large bowl combine the beans with cold water to cover them by at least three inches. Soak overnight. Drain the beans and transfer them to a large, heavy pot. Add fresh cold water to cover them by at least three inches, set over medium heat, and bring to a boil. Lower the heat and simmer, uncovered, stirring once or twice, for 25 minutes. Stir in 2 teaspoons of the salt and continue to cook gently until the beans are just tender, 15 to 25 minutes longer. Drain and transfer to a bowl. In a large skillet over medium heat combine the ham and 3 Tablespoons of the vegetable oil. Cook, tossing and stirring often, until the ham is crisp and brown, 6 to 8 minutes. With a slotted spoon, transfer the ham to the bowl with the beans. Do not clean the pan. Set the skillet over high heat and stir in the maple syrup, cider vinegar, and the remaining vegetable oil. Bring to a boil, stirring and scraping to dissolve any browned bits from the bottom of the skillet. Stir in the thyme, boil 1 minute, and pour the hot dressing over the ham and beans. Add the carrots and stir. Season with the remaining salt and a generous grind of black pepper and stir again. Cool to room temperature, cover, and refrigerate for several hours or overnight. Allow the salad to return to room temperature. Adjust the seasoning. Line plates with the lettuce leaves. Stir the salad and divide it among the plates, shaping each portion into a slight mound. Garnish each salad with the onion. Drizzle any remaining dressing over each salad and serve immediately. Yield: 6 servings.

## Maple Dijon Cream Salad Dressing
• Ingredients
¼ cup extra light olive oil
½ cup salad oil
2-½ Tablespoons Dijon-style mustard
3 Tablespoons dark High Acres maple syrup
2 Tablespoons balsamic vinegar
¼ cup half-and-half
Dash of salt
1 clove garlic, scored
• Preparation
Whisk together all ingredients except the garlic. Add the garlic and let the dressing sit for at least an hour to allow flavors to develop. Add a teaspoon more of vinegar or mustard if you like a sharper taste. The dressing keeps for 4 to 5 days.

## Maple Garlic Vinaigrette
2 large cloves garlic, peeled
1 teaspoon kosher or sea salt
1 Tablespoon Dijon mustard
2 Tablespoons white wine vinegar
1 Tablespoon High Acres maple syrup
1 cup vegetable oil
Freshly ground black pepper, to taste
Puree garlic by chopping it coarsely, sprinkling it with salt, and pressing it with the flat of the knife until you have a relatively smooth paste. In a large bowl, whisk together garlic, mustard, vinegar, and maple syrup. Slowly drizzle in the oil, whisking rapidly all the time, until an emulsion forms and the dressing has a creamy consistency. Add black pepper to taste.

## Maple Ginger Salad Dressing
• Ingredients
4 Tablespoons High Acres maple syrup
2 Tablespoons vegetable oil
2 Tablespoons lemon juice
1 teaspoon ginger, freshly grated
• Preparation: Whisk together the maple syrup, vegetable oil, and lemon juice. Stir in the ginger.

## Maple Herbal Vinaigrette

• Ingredients
⅔ cup olive oil
⅓ cup white wine vinegar
⅓ cup High Acres maple syrup
1 Tablespoon fresh minced chives
1 Tablespoon fresh minced parsley
1 Tablespoon fresh tarragon
• Preparation
Combine all ingredients in blender or processor for 30 seconds.
Chill at least 3 hours before serving.

## Maple Horseradish Salad Dressing (Spicy!)

• Ingredients
2 Tablespoons High Acres maple syrup
1 Tablespoon horseradish sauce
4 Tablespoons red wine vinegar
5 Tablespoons olive oil
1 clove garlic, finely crushed
• Preparation
Mix all ingredients together thoroughly.

## Maple Mustard Vinaigrette

• Ingredients
½ teaspoon salt
¼ teaspoon freshly ground pepper
2 Tablespoons High Acres maple syrup
1 teaspoon Dijon mustard
2 Tablespoons red wine vinegar
½ cup vegetable oil (olive oil is too strong)
• Preparation: Mix together in a jar and shake.

## Spinach Salad with Warm Maple Dressing

Mix together and heat: ½ cup High Acres maple syrup, ¼ to ½
cup cider vinegar (to your taste preference). Pour over 1 pound
washed and dried baby spinach. Add your choice of the
following: bacon crumbles, grated hard boiled egg, grated
cheddar cheese, chopped pecans or walnuts, salt & pepper.

## CHAPTER 14
## SAUCES

### Made-In-Maine Hoisin Sauce
• Ingredients
2 cups High Acres maple syrup
2 cups soy sauce
• Preparation
Place the soy sauce in a medium saucepan and cook down until reduced by one quarter (about 5 minutes). Add the maple syrup and reduce by another quarter. You will do this at fairly high heat taking care not to burn the mix. Put the sauce in a glass jar after it has cooled a bit. Use it on meat and poultry before cooking. You can grill, oven roast or sauté with this sauce. Try savory carrots or caramelize onions in this sauce.

### Maple Barbeque Sauce
• Ingredients
1 cup catsup
1 teaspoon dry mustard
3 Tablespoons Worcestershire Sauce
½ teaspoon onion powder
¼ cup High Acres maple syrup
• Preparation
Mix together. Brush sauce on ribs or chicken. Bake at 350° F until done.

### Maple Glaze for Meats
Just combine
¾ cup High Acres maple syrup
¼ cup apple cider vinegar
1 teaspoon dry mustard
Pinch of ground cloves
Combine in a small saucepan. Bring the mixture to a boil. If you want to glaze meat while it's still roasting in the oven, boil the mixture for a minute or two, because it will thicken further in the oven. If you want to serve the glaze as a sauce, boil it for 3 to 5 minutes so it will thicken.

**Maple Marmalade Sauce**
½ cup High Acres maple syrup
½ cup brown sugar
¼ cup butter, melted
¼ cup marmalade
¼ teaspoon ground nutmeg
● Preparation
Mix ingredients together thoroughly. Serve at room temperature. Store in refrigerator. This sauce is a perfect topping for squash, sweet potatoes, or yams.

*The finished syrup is tested for density, color and flavor.*
*It is then hot-packed at 180°F and labeled.*

**Lobster with Nutmeg Vinaigrette and Chestnut Puree**
• Ingredients
5 (1-¼) pound boiled lobsters, halved
1 cup chicken stock or canned low-sodium broth
1 cup apple cider
2 shallots, minced
1 bay leaf
1 Tablespoon sherry
¼ cup heavy cream
½ teaspoons freshly grated nutmeg
1 Tablespoon vegetable oil
½ small onion, chopped
1 (15-ounce) can whole chestnuts packed in water, drained
2 Tablespoons High Acres maple syrup
1 Tablespoon unsalted butter
¼ cup sour cream (or crème fraîche)
Salt and freshly ground pepper
2 large scallions, chopped
1 Tablespoon chopped parsley
Parsley garnish
• Preparation
In a large saucepan, combine ½ cup of the stock with the cider, shallots, bay leaves and sherry. Boil over high heat until reduced by half, about 25 minutes. Add the heavy cream and nutmeg and simmer over moderate heat until slightly thickened, about 5 minutes. Remove from the heat. In a medium saucepan, heat the vegetable oil. Add the onion and cook over moderate heat until softened. Add the remaining ½ cup of stock and the chestnuts and simmer until the liquid reduces by a third, about 4 minutes. Remove from the heat and add the maple syrup and butter. Transfer the contents of the saucepan to a blender and puree until smooth. Blend in the sour cream or crème fraîche. Transfer the puree to a clean saucepan and season with salt and pepper. Cover and keep warm. Gently reheat the nutmeg vinaigrette. Add the scallions and parsley and season with salt and pepper. Cut the lobster tail meat into 1-inch chunks and replace it in the tail sections of the lobsters.

To serve place one lobster tail and a spoonful of chestnut puree on each plate. Spoon the warm nutmeg vinaigrette over the lobsters and garnish with parsley and serve at once.
Yield: 10 servings

SALMON

## Maple Glazed Salmon
• Ingredients
4 salmon fillets or steaks (6 to 8 oz each)
4 tablespoons High Acres maple syrup
¼ cup white wine
1 Tablespoon minced shallots
3 Cortland apples, pared in wedges
3 to 4 sliced scallions
1 Tablespoon chopped parsley
2 Tablespoons fresh lemon juice
1 teaspoon lemon zest
½ cup flour
3 Tablespoons whole butter
4 Tablespoons clarified butter
Dredge fillets in flour, sauté in skillet with clarified butter 3 minutes per side. Set aside browned fillets, wipe pan. Return pan to burner. Sauté shallots in whole butter only until tender (30-40 seconds). Add wine; reduce by ½ over medium heat. Add lemon juice & maple syrup, boil one minute. Add apple wedges, scallions, parsley, and lemon zest. Cook for about 2 minutes. Arrange fillets on warmed dinner plates and divide apples and glaze over each portion. Serves 4.

## Maple Mustard Salmon
• Ingredients
4 salmon fillets
⅔ cup melted butter
½ Tablespoon dried dill
½ cup maple syrup
¼ cup Dijon style mustard
• Preparation
Blend ingredients over low heat until melted together. Grill or broil salmon, basting and turning until flaky and done.

SCALLOPS

**Broiled and Curried Scallops**
• Ingredients
2 pounds fresh scallops
¼ cup High Acres maple syrup
¼ cup prepared mustard
1 teaspoon lemon juice
1 to 3 teaspoons curry powder, depending on preference
• Preparation
Line broiler pan with foil and arrange scallops in it. Combine syrup, mustard, lemon juice and curry powder. Brush half of this sauce over scallop tops and slide pan under broiler. Broil 5 minutes. Turn scallops and brush with remaining sauce. Broil another 5 minutes.

**Scallops With Bacon and Maple**
• Ingredients
High Acres maple syrup
4 fresh bay scallops
6 slices lean bacon
24 toothpicks soaked in water for 5 minutes
• Preparation
Wrap scallops with bacon and secure with toothpicks. Marinade with High Acres maple syrup. Cover and refrigerate for an hour or more. Broil in oven, basting and turning until crisp on all sides. Drain on paper towel or plate. Arrange on serving platter with fresh parsley and fresh lemon.

*The fourth weekend of March is designated Maine Maple Syrup Weekend. We have a pancake breakfast and sugarhouse open house.*

116

# CHAPTER 16
# SOUPS
## (WHAT GETS US THROUGH THE WINTER IN MAINE)

## Creamed Butternut Squash Apple Soup
- Ingredients
5 pounds butternut squash, peeled and diced
1-½ pounds apples, quartered
1 (1-inch) cinnamon stick
½ gallon chicken stock
1-½ cups unsalted butter (3 sticks)
⅓ cup High Acres maple syrup
½ teaspoon ginger
½ teaspoon salt
½ teaspoon nutmeg
1 pint light cream, hot
- Preparation
Steam the butternut squash, apples, cinnamon and chicken stock together until the squash is soft. Run through a food mill and return to the pot. Add the remaining ingredients except cream and simmer fifteen minutes. Add cream, strain, serve.

## Squash Maple Cream Soup
- Ingredients
1 butternut squash
1 onion, medium (optional)
3 Tablespoons butter
4 cups milk
2 Tablespoons High Acres maple syrup
⅛ teaspoon nutmeg
½ cup heavy cream
- Preparation
Cut squash in half and clean out seeds. Turn upside down in baking dish. Add water to cover bottom of baking dish. Bake in 350°F oven until tender (about 1 hour). Sauté the onion in butter until soft. When squash has cooled, scoop it out and puree in blender with milk and onions until desired consistency. Place in pot; add maple syrup, heavy cream, nutmeg, salt and pepper to taste. Heat to serving temperature and serve immediately.

## CHAPTER 17
## VEGETABLES

BAKED BEANS
There are a gazillion baked bean recipe variations. When I asked people to share maple syrup recipes I was amazed at how many had "secret" family recipes for Baked Beans. Here are the three I like best.

**Traditional Maple Syrup Baked Beans**
• Ingredients
1 pound dry white beans, rinsed and cleaned
6 cups water
6 slices bacon, cut in 2-inch pieces
1 small onion, chopped
½ teaspoon of dry mustard
1-½ teaspoons salt
½ cup dark High Acres maple syrup
2 Tablespoons brown sugar
2 Tablespoons butter
• Preparation
Bring the beans and water to a boil in a large saucepan and boil for 2 minutes. Remove from heat and let stand, covered, for an hour. Return to a boil, and then reduce heat and simmer, covered, for 40 minutes. Drain, reserving cooking liquid. Place half of the bacon in a bean crock, and add beans. In a separate bowl combine the reserved cooking liquid, onion, dry mustard, salt and maple syrup. Pour over the beans and top with remaining bacon. Bake, covered at 325°F for about 3 hours, checking occasionally and adding a bit of water if beans appear dry. Cream together the brown sugar and butter. Sprinkle over the beans and bake, uncovered, an additional hour.

**Baked Beans with Maple, Apples & Rum**
• Ingredients
4 cups dry navy beans
1 lb salt pork or ham
1 cup High Acres maple syrup
1 cup High Acres maple sugar
3 quarts water

1 large onion
1 Tablespoon salt
½ cup butter
1 teaspoon baking soda
1 teaspoon dry mustard
4 apples, cored & unpeeled
½ cup dark rum
• Preparation
Rinse beans, cover with cold water, and soak overnight. Pour beans and water into large pot. Add baking soda and more water to cover beans. Bring to a boil uncovered and boil until some of the skins fall off when you blow on them. Line a bean pot with thin slices of the pork or ham, and pour in beans and water. Roll onion in dry mustard completely and bury it in middle of the beans. Pour maple syrup and salt over top. Bake at 325ºF for 4 to 5 hours. At the start of the last hour, place whole apples on top as close together as possible. Cream maple sugar and butter together and spread over top of apples. Pour rum over top just before serving.

**Easy Way Baked Beans**
• Ingredients
#10 Can of Baked Beans (approx. 3 quarts)
(We use B&M Original because we live in Maine where they are made. And Art knows the guy who maintains their boilers. We have a loyalty there. )
1 cup of the darkest High Acres Maple Syrup we have
• Preparation
Mix in the maple syrup and heat through. This gets better the longer you heat it. I use a crock pot.

GARDEN VEGGIES

**Apple and Red Cabbage Casserole**
• Ingredients
1 chopped apple
1 medium onion, sliced
¼ cup water
⅓ cup apple cider vinegar
¼ cup brown sugar (maple sugar)

Fresh ginger about the size of a quarter (or a dash of ground ginger)
4 cups shredded red cabbage (1 medium)
Salt and pepper to taste
• Preparation
Sauté onion and apple in a little oil in a Dutch oven or frying pan until tender. Add all remaining ingredients. Cover and cook until tender, about 1 hour. Serve hot or cold

## Brussels Sprouts in Maple Glaze
• Ingredients
3 cups white onions, small, peeled
3 cups Brussels sprouts, small
½ cup High Acres maple syrup
2 Tablespoons tarragon vinegar
3 cups canned chestnuts
½ teaspoon black pepper
• Preparation
With a small knife, cut an x into the root ends of the onions and the Brussels sprouts. In a large pot of boiling water, blanch onions for 3-4 minutes. Remove with a slotted spoon and place in a medium-sized bowl. Blanch Brussels sprouts in the same water for 3-4 minutes. Pour into a colander; let cool, and set aside. In a 3-quart saucepan, warm maple syrup for 4 minutes over medium–high heat. Add the vinegar and onions. Reduce heat and simmer until the liquid has almost evaporated. 20-30 minutes. Add chestnuts and Brussels sprouts; stir and cook until sprouts are heated but still bright green, about 5 minutes. Season with pepper.

## Carrots with Maple Glaze
Boil baby carrots (or full size carrots that have been cut into julienne slices) in water for about 10 minutes. Meanwhile, melt butter or use olive oil in a skillet. Drain the carrots, and sauté in the skillet for 5-10 minutes, adding some High Acres maple syrup and heat until the carrots are glazed. You can add herbs or spices for a variation. I like dill, celery seed, ginger or cardamom. (Pick one.) You can also use sliced sweet potatoes instead of carrots. The longer the carrots sit in the mixture, the better they taste.

## Maple-Rum Roasted Root Vegetables
• Ingredients
3 medium carrots, peeled and cut into 1-¼ inch chunks
3 medium parsnips, peeled and cut into 1-¼ inch chunks
1 small (½ pound) yellow turnip
3-4 medium potatoes, cut into sticks (like French Fries)
½ cup High Acres maple syrup
¼ cup bourbon or rum
1-½ teaspoons course salt
 Freshly ground black pepper
• Preparation
Preheat oven to 350ºF. Arrange the carrots, parsnips, turnip and potatoes in a single layer in a shallow roasting pan. Heat the butter and maple syrup in a small saucepan just until the butter is melted, about 2 minutes. Remove from heat. Stir in the rum. Pour the maple mixture over the vegetables and toss to thoroughly coat. Sprinkle the vegetables with the salt and pepper to taste. Cover the pan with aluminum foil and bake for 25 minutes. Remove the pan from the oven; stir the vegetables, and bake, uncovered, until tender, 20 to 25 minutes longer.

POTATOES AND RICE

## Potatoes, Mashed and Made Fancy
• Ingredients
20 good-sized potatoes, peeled
¾ cup unsalted butter
2 to 3 cups milk
2 Tablespoons High Acres maple syrup
¾ cup Parmesan cheese
Salt and freshly ground black pepper
¼ teaspoon dry thyme (scant Tablespoon, minced, if using fresh thyme leaves)
½ teaspoon dry sage leaves (1 small handful, minced, if using fresh sage leaves)
½ teaspoon dry savory leaves (2 teaspoons, minced, if using fresh savory leaves)
• Preparation

Place the potatoes in a large stockpot and cover with 2 inches of water. Add 1 teaspoon of salt, bring to a boil over high heat, and boil just until the potatoes are soft but not mushy. Drain the potatoes and transfer to an electric mixer fitted with a whisk. Gradually add the milk, adding enough so the potatoes are soft but not runny. The amount will vary depending on the variety and age of the potatoes. With the beater running, add the syrup, and the cheese, mixing well. Add the herbs to the potatoes, mixing well. Season to taste with salt and pepper. Keep warm until serving. Makes 10 to 12 servings.

**Wild Rice With Cherries and Hazelnuts**
• Ingredients
1 cup wild rice
2-½ cups water
¼ teaspoon salt
High Acres maple syrup
½ cup dried cherries (or cranberries)
½ cup chopped, lightly toasted hazelnuts (also called filberts)
Milk or cream
• Preparation
Place the wild rice, water, and salt in a medium-sized saucepan and bring to a boil over medium heat. When it reaches a boil, cover the pot, and lower the heat to a bare simmer. Cook for 1-¼ hours, or until all the water is absorbed and the rice is tender and has "butterflied," or burst open. (If the grain has become tender but there is still water left, drain it off.) Remove from the heat, and stir in the maple syrup and the cherries. Serve hot, topped with chopped hazelnuts and milk. Yield: 3 to 4 servings

SQUASH, SWEET POTATOES AND YAMS

**Acorn Squash Stuffed with Apple Couscous**
• Ingredients
1 cup couscous
1 cup apple juice
¼ cup prunes, pitted and chopped
¼ cup dried cranberries
¼ cup dried apple
¼ cup apple juice concentrate, thawed

¼ teaspoon cardamom, ground
1 Tablespoon High Acres maple syrup
4 acorn squash, halved and seeded
¼ cup pecans or walnuts, toasted and chopped (optional)
• Preparation
Place couscous in a small mixing bowl and set aside. Bring apple juice to a boil in a small saucepan and pour over the couscous. Cover and set aside until the juice is absorbed. This will take 15 minutes. Stir in the fruit, apple juice concentrate, cardamom, and maple syrup. Set aside. Steam squash halves until tender, about 15 minutes. Drain and place on a baking sheet. Preheat oven to 350ºF. Fill squash halves with the couscous mixture and bake for 20 minutes. Top with nuts, if desired, and serve. Yield: 8 servings

## Buttercup Squash with Apple Stuffing
• Ingredients
4 buttercup or acorn squash
1 large apple, chopped
⅓ cup walnuts, chopped
¼ cup sugar
¼ cup raisins
2 Tablespoons butter
¼ cup High Acres maple syrup
• Preparation
Preheat oven to 400°F. Wash squash. Cut tops off and scrape out seeds and strings. Bake face down on baking sheet until squash is tender when pricked with fork. Combine remaining ingredients in saucepan and heat gently until well blended and soft. When squash is done remove from oven and fill cavities with filling. Pour a little maple syrup over each top, just to moisten and return to oven to heat through.

## Butternut Squash with Maple Rum Glaze
• Ingredients
1 medium butternut squash
4 Tablespoons High Acres maple syrup
¼ teaspoon ground mace
4 Tablespoons dark rum
⅔ cup water

• Preparation

Peel the squash, and remove the seeds. Quarter it and cut into half inch slices. Place all ingredients in a large saucepan. Bring to a boil, then simmer for 15 minutes, or until the squash is tender. Reserving the cooking liquid, transfer the squash with a slotted spoon to a heated serving dish. Boil the cooking liquid until it is thickened, then pour it over the squash. Serves 4

**Captain Art's Microwave Acorn Squash**

Preheat the whole Acorn Squash in the microwave for 1 minute on high. Cut in half, remove the seeds and membranes. Place the flesh side down in ¼ cup of orange juice (or water) and microwave on high for approximately 8-10 minutes, or until tender. Turn over when fork tender. Drizzle with butter and maple syrup.

**Maple Glazed Yams with Orange and Cranberries**

• Ingredients

4-¾ pounds of yams (sweet potatoes), peeled, and cut into 1" pieces
¾ cup High Acres maple syrup
6 Tablespoons (¾ stick) butter, melted
1-½ teaspoons orange peel
6 Tablespoons dried cranberries (Ocean Spray calls them Craisins, and they also market orange flavored dried cranberries and cherry flavored dried cranberries.)
Chopped fresh parsley

• Preparation

Preheat oven to 350°F. Cook yams in large pot of boiling salted water for 3 minutes. Drain and transfer to a 13"x 9"x 2" glass baking dish. Blend syrup, butter and peel in small bowl. Pour over yams. Sprinkle with salt and pepper, toss to coat. (Can be made 1 day ahead. Cover and refrigerate). Cooking time is 60 minutes. Makes 8 to 10 servings

**Squash Casserole for a Church Supper**

• Ingredients

2 lb. squash (Hubbard or Buttercup) cooked and mashed
2 Tablespoons High Acres maple syrup
1 medium onion, chopped fine

1 cup shredded carrot
1 cup sour cream
Small can cream of chicken soup
8 oz. package prepared bread stuffing mix
• Preparation
Prepare squash. In small mixing bowl, combine onion, carrot, sour cream, maple syrup and soup. Fold into squash. Prepare stuffing as directed and spread half in bottom of 12"x 7"x 2" baking. Spoon squash mixture on top. Sprinkle with remaining stuffing.

## Sweet Potatoes With Maple
• Ingredients
½ cup High Acres maple syrup
2 pounds sweet potatoes, peeled and sliced thin
¼ cup orange juice
2 Tablespoons High Acres maple sugar
2 Tablespoons of stick butter, melted
½ teaspoon salt
¼ cup chopped, toasted walnuts
⅛ teaspoon ground cloves
• Preparation
Mix syrup, juice, maple sugar, butter, salt, and cloves. Pour over sweet potatoes in the bottom of a casserole dish. Cover with plastic wrap and microwave on high for 10 minutes. Uncover and microwave on high for 5 more minutes or until potato is done. Sprinkle with walnuts.

## Whipped Sweet Potatoes with Apples
• Ingredients
3-½ pounds sweet potatoes, about 6 medium
2 Tablespoons plus 2 teaspoons unsalted butter or margarine
2 Tablespoons High Acres dark maple syrup
Salt and freshly ground black pepper
1 apple (I use Golden Delicious)
• Preparation
Preheat oven to 400ºF. Grease an 8-inch baking. Melt 2 teaspoons butter in a cup in the microwave. Bake sweet potatoes until soft, 40-60 minutes, depending on size. Peel as soon as they are cool enough to handle. Place the flesh of

potatoes in food processor or large bowl. Add remaining 2 Tablespoons butter and maple syrup to hot sweet potatoes. Process to puree, or mash with a fork, until smooth, season lightly with salt and pepper. Spread in prepared baking dish, making an even layer. Peel, halve and core apple, slice into thin slices. Arrange slices over the sweet potatoes. Brush apples lightly with the melted butter. Bake, uncovered until yams are heated through and apples have softened, 25 to 30 minutes. Yield: 8 servings

## Winter Squash Casserole
• Ingredients
14 cups winter squash cooked and cubed (or buy it canned or frozen).
Combine the following and add to the squash:
½ cup Half & Half
½ cup High Acres dark maple syrup
1 teaspoon vanilla
¾ teaspoon salt
1 egg, beaten
Beat with mixer and spoon into a greased 9" x 13" pan.
Combine the following:
½ cup flour
½ cup brown sugar
¼ cup butter
Then stir in ½ cup chopped pecans or walnuts
• Preparation
Spread over top of squash mixture and cover. Bake at 375°F for 15 minutes. Uncover and bake an additional 25 minutes. Sweet potatoes can be used in place of squash.

# CHAPTER 18
## MISCELLANEOUS AND MEDICINALS

### All-Season Maple Suet for the Birds
• Ingredients
1 cup crunchy peanut butter
1 cup lard (no substitutes)
2 cups oatmeal
2 cups corn meal
1 cup whole wheat flour
½ cup High Acres maple syrup
• Preparation: Melt the lard and peanut butter. Stir in remaining ingredients. Pour mixture into 9"x 9" pan (1-½" thick). Allow cooling, cut into squares. Store in freezer.

### Herbal Maple Cough Drops
(Ben, this one's for you!)
6 cups High Acres maple syrup (light amber preferred)
2 cups corn syrup
2 large handfuls White Pine Bark curls, dried
1 handful Blue Violet leaves and flowers, dried
1 handful of Coltsfoot leaves, dried
1 handful of Mullein leaves, dried
Place herbs together in a crock pot. Cover the herbs with the syrup. Put a tight fitting lid on the crock pot and let sit for a couple of days to infuse the medicinal properties of the herbs into the syrup. Strain the syrup through cheesecloth to remove the plant material. Wring the cheesecloth around your hand. Cook infused syrup on the stove, and use a high-sided pot with a spout. It will foam but do not use de-foamer. If the pan is deep enough it should not foam over. Don't stir. Heat to 280°Fdegrees. Pour by droplets onto waxed paper

### High Acres Cold Remedy
1 part High Acres maple syrup
1 part lemon juice
2 parts whiskey
4 parts water or crushed ice
Combine all ingredients and shake well. Go to bed and sip slowly!

# RECIPE INDEX

Maple Sugar Candy 48
Pumpkin Candy 52
Captain Art's Microwave Acorn Squash 124
Captain Art's Shipwreck Sundae 73
CARAMEL Maple Caramel Candy Pie 75
CARROT
Carrots with Maple Glaze 120
Maple Oatmeal Carrot Muffins 29
Maple Rum Roasted Root Vegetables 121
Root Vegetable Quick Bread 28
CEREAL Maple Granola 37
CHEESE
Monte Cristo French Toast 39
Whipped Maple Mascarpone 46
CHEESECAKE
Maple Praline Cheesecake 68
Maple Pumpkin Cheesecake 68
Maple Walnut Cheesecake 69
CHERRY
Maple Cherry Topping 45
Wild Rice With Cherries and Hazelnuts 122
CHESTNUT Lobster with Nutmeg Vinaigrette and Chestnut Puree 114
Chewy Maple Coconut Cookies Like Gramma Made 53
CHICKEN
Chicken Breasts with Maple Horseradish Glaze 100
Chicken Breasts with Maple Mustard Sauce 100
Chicken in Maple Cream 100
Chicken Thighs with Maple Barbeque Glaze 101
Chicken with Golden Curry Sauce 101
Grilled Breast of Chicken with Maple-Bourbon Glaze 102
Grilled Chicken with Maple Sauce 102
Maple Chicken with Lemon and Almonds 103
Maple Sweet & Sour Chicken 103
Rosemary Chicken with Orange-Maple Glaze 104
Spicy Chicken Wings 105
Chicken in Maple Cream 100
Chicken Thighs with Maple Barbeque Glaze 101
Chicken with Golden Curry Sauce 101
CHOCOLATE
Chocolate Tofu Grand Marnier Pudding 80
Frozen Maple Chocolate Marshmallow Delight 70
Frozen Maple Walnut Mousse Pie 71
CIDER Hot Maple Cider 19
Cinnamon Maple Ring Cookies 53
COCKTAIL
Oak Hill Farm Sleigh Ride Cocktail 19
Sugarbush Cocktail 20
COCONUT

Maple Lemon Pineapple Cake (from a Mix) 63
Lemon-Maple Zucchini Quick Bread 24
LIMA BEAN Ham and Lima Bean Salad with Maple Thyme Dressing 108
Lobster with Nutmeg Vinaigrette and Chestnut Puree 114
LOLLIPOPS Maple Lollipops 51
Low-Cal Maple Milk 17
Maple Sesame Milk 17
Made-In-Maine Hoisin Sauce 112
Maine Maple Dumplings 85
aple Apple Crunch 75
Maple Apple Muffins 28
Maple Apple Stuffing for Crown Roast of Pork 95
Maple Applesauce Topping 45
Maple Barbecue Sauce 112
Maple Barbecued Pork Spareribs 95
Maple Beef (or Venison) Jerky 15
Maple Bread Pudding 80
Maple Breakfast Biscuits 33
Maple Butter 90
Maple Caramel Candy Pie 75
Maple Charlotte 81
Maple Cherry Topping 45
Maple Chicken with Lemon and Almonds 103
Maple Cocktail Sausage Spears 12
Maple Cookie Rollup 55
Maple Corn Muffins 30
Maple Cornbread 25
Maple Cream 90
Maple Cream Cheese Spread 90
Maple Cream Filling for Cakes, Cream Puffs or Twinkies 70
Maple Crème Brulee 82
Maple Custard 81
Maple Date Walnut Quick Bread 25
Maple Dijon Cream Salad Dressing 110
Maple Frosting 70
Maple Fruit Meringues 55
Maple Fudge 50
Maple Garlic Vinaigrette 110
Maple Ginger Cake 60
Maple Ginger Ice Cream 72
Maple Ginger Salad Dressing 110
Maple Glaze for Meats 112
Maple Glazed Coconut Walnut Rolls 36
Maple Glazed Pumpkin Ring 61
Maple Glazed Salmon 115
Maple Glazed Yams with Orange and Cranberries 124
Maple Granola 37
Maple Hazelnut Coffee Cake 62

Maple Herbal Vinaigrette 111
Maple Hermits 56
Maple Horseradish Salad Dressing (Spicy!) 111
Maple Ice Cream Pie 72
Maple Jelly 91
Maple Lemon Pineapple Cake (from a Mix) 63
Maple Lollipops 51
Maple Marmalade Sauce 113
Maple Mustard Pork Tenderloin 96
Maple Mustard Salmon 115
Maple Mustard Vinaigrette 111
Maple Nut Brittle 51
Maple Nut Butter Frosting 70
Maple Oatmeal Carrot Muffins 29
Maple Oatmeal Walnut Muffins 30
Maple on Snow "Leather Aprons" 51
Maple Orange Cranberry Relish 91
Maple Peanut Butter Topping 46
Maple Pecan Divinity 48
Maple Pecan Pie 76
Maple Pecan Scones 32
Maple Pecan Squares 56
Maple Pie 77
Maple Pork Chops 96
Maple Praline Cheesecake 68
Maple Pralines 48
Maple Pumpkin Apple Cookies 57
Maple Pumpkin Cake 63
Maple Pumpkin Cheesecake 68
Maple Raisin Quick Bread 26
Maple Rhubarb Pie 77
Maple Rice Pudding 82
Maple Roasted Turkey with Riesling Wine Gravy 106
Maple Rum Roasted Root Vegetables 121
Maple Rye Yeast Bread 21
Maple Sesame Milk 17
Maple Spice Cake 64
Maple Spice Glazed Duck Breasts 105
Maple Sponge Cake 64
Maple Sticky Rolls (A Yeast Bread) 33
Maple Sticky Rolls from Frozen Bread Dough 35
Maple Sugar Candy 48
Maple Sugar Cookies 57
Maple Sweet & Sour Chicken 103
Maple Toasted Walnuts 83
Maple Walnut Bran Muffins 29
Maple Walnut Pull Apart Bread (A Yeast Bread) 22
Maple Walnut Cheesecake 69

Maple Walnut Coconut Bars 54
Maple Walnut Ice Cream 73
Maple Walnut Parfait 82
Maple Walnut Yogurt Muffins 31
Maple Whole Wheat Quick Bread 26
Maple with Ham Appetizer Biscuits 12
MARSHMALLOW Frozen Maple Chocolate Marshmallow Delight 70
MASCARPONE Whipped Maple Mascarpone 46
Mashed Maple Syrup Apples 87
MEDICINALS
    Herbal Maple Cough Drops 127
    High Acres Cold Remedy 127
MERINGUES Maple Fruit Meringues 55
Microwave Maple Pudding 83
Monte Cristo French Toast 39
MOUSSE
    Frozen Maple Mousse 71
    Frozen Maple Walnut Mousse Pie 71
    Oak Hill Farm Maple Mousse 83
    Simple Maple Mousse 84
MUFFINS
    Maple Apple Muffins 28
    Maple Corn Muffins 30
    Maple Oatmeal Carrot Muffins 29
    Maple Oatmeal Walnut Muffins 30
    Maple Walnut Bran Muffins 29
    Maple Walnut Yogurt Muffins 31
Nutty Whole Wheat Cinnamon Pancakes 43
Oak Hill Farm Maple Mousse 83
Oak Hill Farm Sleigh Ride Cocktail 19
OATMEAL
    Doug Chapman's Oatmeal Maple Bread 21
    Maple Granola 37
    Maple Oatmeal Carrot Muffins 29
    Maple Oatmeal Walnut Muffins 30
    Oatmeal Maple Pancakes 44
    Oatmeal Raisin Walnut Cookies 58
Old-Time Maple Gingerbread 65
ORANGE
    Chocolate Tofu Grand Marnier Pudding 80
    Maple Marmalade Sauce 113
    Maple Orange Cranberry Relish 91
    Maple-Glazed Yams with Orange and Cranberries 124
    Orange Fig Walnut Topping 45
    Orange Maple Walnut Quick Bread 27
    Oranges with Maple Carmel 87
    Rosemary Chicken with Orange-Maple Glaze 104
    Summer Fruit Compote 88

RHUBARB
    Maple Rhubarb Pie 77
    Rhubarb Maple-Ginger Punch 17
RICE
    Maple Rice Pudding 82
    Wild Rice With Cherries and Hazelnuts 122
ROLLS
    Maple Glazed Coconut Walnut Rolls
    Maple Sticky Rolls (A Yeast Bread) 33
    Maple Sticky Rolls from Frozen Bread Dough 35
Root Vegetable Quick Bread 28
Rosemary Chicken with Orange-Maple Glaze 104
RYE Maple Rye Yeast Bread 21
SALAD
    Coleslaw the Way We Do It In Maine 108
    Ham and Lima Bean Salad with Maple Thyme Dressing 108
    Spinach Salad with Warm Maple Dressing 111
SALAD DRESSING
    Fruit Salad Dressing 108
    Maple Dijon Cream Salad Dressing 110
    Maple Garlic Vinaigrette 110
    Maple Ginger Salad Dressing 110
    Maple Herbal Vinaigrette 111
    Maple Horseradish Salad Dressing (Spicy!) 111
    Maple Mustard Vinaigrette 111
SALMON
    Maple Glazed Salmon 115
    Maple Mustard Salmon 115
SAUCE
    Made-In-Maine Hoisin Sauce 112
    Maple Barbecue Sauce 112
    Maple Glaze for Meats 112
    Maple Marmalade Sauce 113
SAUSAGE Maple Cocktail Sausage Spears 12
SCALLOPS
    Broiled and Curried Scallops 116
    Scallops with Bacon & Maple Cream 13
    Scallops With Bacon and Maple 116
SCONES
    Frosted Maple Scones 31
    Maple Pecan Scones 32
SHISH KEBAB
    Pork Tenderloin Maple Syrup Shish Kebabs 99
    Beef Maple Teriyaki Skewers 14
Simple Maple Mousse 84
SKEWER
    Pork Tenderloin Maple Syrup Shish Kebabs 99
    Beef Maple Teriyaki Skewers 14

Soft Almond Maple Cookies 58
SOUP
      Creamed Butternut Squash Apple Soup 117
      Squash/Maple Cream Soup 117
SPARERIBS
      Crispy Maple Spareribs 94
      Maple Barbecued Pork Spareribs 95
      Pork Spareribs in Maple Syrup 98
      Spicy Chicken Wings 105
Spinach Salad with Warm Maple Dressing 111
SPONGE CAKE Maple Sponge Cake 64
SPREAD
      Maple Butter 90
      Maple Cream 90
      Maple Cream Cheese Spread 90
SQUASH
      Acorn Squash Stuffed with Apple Couscous 122
      Buttercup Squash with Apple Stuffing 123
      Butternut Squash with Maple Rum Glaze 123
      Captain Art's Microwave Acorn Squash 124
      Creamed Butternut Squash Apple Soup 117
      Lemon-Maple Zucchini Quick Bread 24
      Pumpkin Candy 52
      Squash Casserole for a Church Supper 124
      Squash/Maple Cream Soup 117
      Winter Squash Casserole 126
Strawberry Cooler 18
Streusel Pecan Squares 59
STUFFING  Maple-Apple Stuffing for Crown Roast of Pork 95
Sue Melanson's Maple Syrup Apple Pie 78
SUET All-Season Suet for the Birds 127
SUGAR ON SNOW
      Maple on Snow "Leather Aprons" 51
      Sugarhouse Sugar-On-Snow Cake 65
Sugarbush Cocktail 20
Sugarhouse Sugar-On-Snow Cake 65
Summer Fruit Compote 88
SWEET AND SOUR Maple Sweet & Sour Chicken 103
SWEET POTATOES
      Maple-Glazed Yams with Orange and Cranberries 124
      Sweet Potatoes With Maple 125
      Whipped Sweet Potatoes with Apples 125
TAFFY Maple on Snow "Leather Aprons" 51
TERIYAKI Beef Maple Teriyaki Skewers 14
Thick Maple Milkshake 18
Three-Flour Buttermilk Pancakes 44
TOFU Chocolate Tofu Grand Marnier Pudding 80
TOPPING

*Sugar Maple identification*    *Red Maple identification*

## ABOUT THE AUTHOR

Susan Chapman Melanson graduated from Miss Teed's English class at Wellesley High School in Massachusetts; Colby Junior College (now called Colby Sawyer College) in NH; and Hiram College in Ohio. Melanson and her husband, Capt. Art Melanson, a retired oil tanker captain, grew up together in Wellesley, MA and reconnected in time to celebrate their 50th birthdays together. Just prior to moving to Maine, Sue lived in Reading, MA for 14 years as Sue Horn. In 1995 Art and Sue bought Oak Hill Farm in the foothills of the White Mountains and began the adventure they are living today.

Mrs. Melanson is an author, a newspaper reporter, an herbalist, a shamanic healer, the class historian for her high school class, and an advocate for breast cancer awareness. The Melansons owned and operated a sled dog kennel when they first came to South Hiram that gave their road the name Husky Haven. The kennel has been phased out as the dogs (and the owners) became older. Now they put their energies into three overnight rental cottages that they built from the ground up, as well as a substantial maple syrup operation that was the reason for collecting the recipes offered in this book.

### OTHER BOOKS BY THIS AUTHOR

"Wentworth By The Sea, 1969 ~ A Novel" (Xlibris.com 2000)

"Nepal: Three Weeks of Cultural & Shamanic Immersion, April 2006" (Lulu.com 2006)

"Confessions of the Classmate Who Never Was,
Northfield School for Girls Class of 1964" (Lulu.com 2006)

"Radiation Buddies"
Melanson, Susan Chapman and Archie Campbell (Lulu.com 2007)

www.ingramcontent.com/pod-product-compliance
Lightning Source LLC
Chambersburg PA
CBHW032003040426
42448CB00006B/477